Ready to Learn

From Birth to School Readiness

Martyn Rawson
and Michael Rose

Hawthorn Press

Ready to Learn © Copyright 2002 Martyn Rawson and Michael Rose

Martyn Rawson and Michael Rose are hereby identified as authors of this work in accordance with Section 77 of the Copyright, Designs and Patent Act, 1988. They assert and give notice of their moral right under this Act.

Published by Hawthorn Press, Hawthorn House, 1 Lansdown Lane, Stroud, Gloucestershire, GL5 1BJ, UK
Tel: (01453) 757040 Fax: (01453) 751138
info@hawthornpress.com
www.hawthornpress.com

Cover photograph by Emma Aylett
Cover design by Hawthorn Press
Typeset at Hawthorn Press by Lynda Smith
Printed in the UK by The Cromwell Press, Trowbridge, Wiltshire

Grateful acknowledgment to:
Rudolf Steiner Press, Sussex for the illustrations from *Understanding Children's Drawings* by Michaela Strauss

Every effort has been made to trace the ownership of all copyrighted material. If any omission has been made, please bring this to the publisher's attention so that proper acknowledgment may be given in future editions.

British Library Cataloguing in Publication Data applied for

ISBN 1 903458 15 3

Contents

Introduction

by Dr John Pearce

Anyone who regularly observes children will have become increasingly aware that all is not well with young people today. Is this just an impression – is this simply a case of 'things were not like this when I was a child'? The research evidence suggests that there has been a real change for the worse in the more 'developed' countries. These studies have to take into account changes in social attitude and expectations as well as changes in diagnostic criteria. The reported increase in Autism is probably due to the latter and the rise in cases of Attention Deficit and Hyperactivity Disorder may be due to a combination of a lower threshold for making the diagnosis and a change in social attitude towards child development and training.

There is good evidence for a real rise in childhood depression and suicide in young men. An increasing number of children in the UK are expelled from school at a young age and disruptive and disobedient behaviour presents teachers and parents with ever more demanding challenges.

I have noticed these changes in my own clinical work with children and have been particularly struck by the difficulty that many parents seem to have nowadays in very basic childcare tasks. Our modern world is not child friendly place, but there is much that can be done to improve things. *Ready to Learn* is an excellent starting point for both teachers and parents. Here is an understanding of child development and the ever-changing needs of maturing children that is unusually detailed and insightful. The authors have combined their knowledge and experience in a way that provides a special combination of knowledge, wisdom and practical guidelines. The reader will find the book thought provoking and may not agree with everything in it. My advice would be to try out the ideas and see for yourself.

Dr John Pearce FRCP, FRCPsych, FRCHPaed, MPhil, DCH
Professor Emeritus in Child and Adolescent Psychiatry,
Nottingham University

Foreword

by John Burnett

The shelves of University libraries are well-stocked with books on child development and the ways children learn. Adjoining these are texts on the ways teachers and parents can help children realise their own potential. At first glance *Ready to Learn* might appear to be one more book to add to the store but closer examination will show that this is a book with a difference. It is a book on *readiness*, with a distinct focus on the ideas and methods practised by teachers in Steiner Waldorf schools.

The authors have many years experience as Steiner Waldorf educators, working within an educational system which emphasises a developmental approach to curriculum and methodology. The scope of this little book, however, reaches far beyond a single perspective. It is rich with stimulating and challenging ideas derived from good practice and contemporary research into the subject. It is written in a style easily accessible to parents and non-specialists but has much to offer serious students of education. I welcome this publication as an important addition to a vital but somewhat neglected field of study.

John Burnett, BA (Hons) Waldorf Steiner Education,
Programme Director, Rolle School of Education,
University of Plymouth

1. This Book

This book is about the way young children learn and how best they can develop and realize their potential. We shall not, however, be promoting the fashionable 'hot house' approach to early learning. Our intention is very much the opposite. We want to show that the premature intellectual awakening of children runs counter to their real long-term interests.

Our discussion points ultimately toward the question, 'When is a child ready to go to school?'. In order to answer this question we must first establish what a child needs to learn in its pre-school years. This early developmental learning phase is *the essential foundation* upon which all future education must stand, totter, or fall. The bulk of our book will be devoted to an illumination of its significance. We shall then consider when and how a transition is made into formal schooling, in the different contexts of home, pre-school, and school proper.

Why Is This So Important?

Compared with 25 years ago, today's children display a worrying rise in nervousness, stress, and hyperactivity. The drug Ritalin is being administered like a behavioural aspirin to a whole generation of children, sweeping some of the troublesome symptoms under the carpet but doing nothing about the causes.

There is an increase in eating and sleeping disorders, in eczema, asthma, and other allergies. There is also growing evidence of impaired speech development and various other characteristics typical of the 'autistic spectrum'. Dyslexia is on the increase. In general we are seeing ever more children in need of developmental and learning support.

And How about the 'Normal' Children?

We all know of youngsters who come home from early education so tired that they are ready for little more than pyjamas and bed. On 'day one' of the educational process it is already possible to observe the loss of innocence of some children. As time goes by, this may develop into a deep disappointment and 'turning off', which can take all sorts of forms. Boys in particular are suffering from their failure to engage early on in what education has to offer.

The explanation for these phenomena is obviously to be found in the 'big picture' of the times we live in. Diet, medications, life-style, family situations, opportunities, expectations, and ambitions – all these are relevant. But one thing is certain: the key to making improvements must be found in the way we understand and treat our children, above all in the first years of their lives.

Our book will try to make clearer how children learn to make sense of themselves and the world. It will also assert strongly that childhood can be, and should be, a time where physical, emotional, and intellectual development can be in harmony, woven together as are themes in music. Parents, wider family, friends, carers, and teachers all have a part to play in this harmony. As with good music, there is a beautiful immediacy to the way childhood naturally unfolds. There is also complexity and profundity to the human being. By overlooking or understating this complexity we may still get some seductive ideas – but with no guarantee that they will translate into healthy and effective practice, as contemporary experience shows only too clearly.

The insights on which this book is based come from a wide range of observation and research, but most directly from the authors' personal experiences as parents and teachers within the international educational movement pioneered in 1919 by Rudolf Steiner – the Steiner Waldorf schools movement. One of the distinguishing features of these schools is that they take child development as their starting point and model their curriculum and educational approach around it. Children are encouraged but not pushed to learn, and the learning process itself is a fully integrated one that offers a complete education to every child. Steiner's exposition of the developing human being has proven to be fruitful in its practical applications for some 80 years. It is gratifying to acknowledge that many of his illuminations have been substantiated and accepted by representatives of current mainstream opinion – although no less disappointing that so much has also been overlooked or disregarded.

We hope that what we have to say about children will be accessible to anyone with real, day-to-day experience of children themselves. While we shall indeed make reference to different researchers and collections of evidence to give weight to our discussion, we have not set out primarily to write an 'academic' book. We are concerned less to prove a point than to open up a question – a question that belongs with the language of common sense, and that is every child-oriented adult's business. If our readers are encouraged to search further for the 'proof that is in the pudding', we believe that our book will have given them a good start, and thereby have achieved its purpose.

2. Early Learning Options

Different countries have evolved a variety of educational systems with their own teaching methods, curricula, and age brackets. These distinctions are most striking in the realm of early years education. Broadly speaking, the central European and Scandinavian countries have followed the lead set by Hungary and Switzerland in the first half of the nineteenth century in placing great emphasis on 'kindergarten' education and clearly distinguishing this from 'primary' education. The typical kindergarten provision in these countries was, and has largely remained, non-academic and play orientated. Children only make the transition to formal '3Rs' learning in their sixth or even seventh year.

A similar focus appears in countries further east. Even 'go-ahead' Japan adopted the Hungarian model in the 1880s and then revitalized it as a key to national development in the 1970s. Australia and New Zealand begin their formal education at six and five respectively, but have both recently sent representatives to Hungary to study that kindergarten model in action.

In Europe, formal schooling begins earlier than six in Greece, Luxembourg, The Netherlands, and the United Kingdom. The twentieth century closed with the explicit development of literacy and numeracy being firmly nailed, in the British mainstream, to the four-year-old's agenda. In the United States, enough alarm bells had sounded in time to draw the line, for most states, at the fifth year.

The impulse to give children an early start in education follows from the notion that this will benefit them academically, and later professionally; and that a 'first-off-the-blocks' nation will be more likely to prosper. We live in an ultra-competitive world, and the accelerated learning idea is extremely persuasive – especially when supported by evidence that children *can* learn early. However, history is already beginning to indicate that this great idea is not so great after all: that 'head start' in theory is developing into 'head over heels' in practice. Enough time has passed for the longer-term outcomes of the early learning approach to be better assessed and put into context. There have also been new findings on how children's learning processes develop biologically in the early years that confirm the dangers of trying to accelerate or specialize natural developmental timetables. (More on this later.)

A British television documentary (Channel 4's Dispatches – *'Two Much Too Soon'*, 1998) brought this whole question strongly into the public consciousness. Two particularly impressive bodies of evidence were referred to by the programme makers, David and Clare Mills. One was a large control study (involving 10,000 children) conducted in Hungary in the 1970s, which focused on the different outcomes obtained from teaching children to write either before or after their sixth year. The other was a longitudinal study undertaken over 30 years in the USA, known as the *High/Scope* Project. In this experiment children aged 3-4 years from the same disadvantaged background were given three alternative forms of early education (allocated randomly):

- an academically orientated 'direct-instruction' schooling
- a loosely structured, play-orientated traditional nursery school
- a child-initiated 'learning through doing' approach represented by the High/Scope scheme itself.

The progress of these children has been monitored ever since. Some of the results of the study are summarized at the end of this chapter.

Based on these two studies and on other evidence, the conclusions of the Channel 4 documentary were substantial and unequivocal. They were, quite simply, that children receive at most a short-term academic benefit from an early introduction to academic schooling. In the medium and longer term, these early-start children not only lose their early academic advantage; they also, in later life, give clear evidence of being less personally satisfied with their lives and (judged starkly by available crime figures) less socially integrated.

Further support for a cautionary approach to early formal education came from the BBC's *Panorama* programme, *'Failing at Four'*, which appeared the following year. This documentary opened with the question: 'Is too much too young causing our children to fail?'. The focus of the programme was a boy, Max Harris, who, at the beginning of filming, was two weeks away from starting in an English primary school at the age of 4. The programme followed his progress over the following year and then set this in the context of the 'later start' approaches taken by other countries, in particular Norway. Reference was also made to the High/Scope Project, to a study done in Portugal, and, closer to home, to a provisional study undertaken by the British Government's Early Years Research Project – all of which supported the view that to educate children 'too much too soon' was at best misguided, and at worst counterproductive and damaging.

The special impact of *'Failing at Four'* was that it pictured an individual transformation, brought about within a single year, of a healthy, happy, normal child into a visibly anxious, fractious, thumb-sucking boy for whom school had become a cloud over the sun. There was nothing about Max, his family, or his school to make this transformation an exceptional case within the broad band of 'advantaged' children attending a decent state primary school. His parents' comments about his 'decline' were echoed by others who were interviewed. Readers' letters that appeared subsequently in Britain's newspapers confirmed the impression that Max's experience was commonplace. For those less advantaged children, with parents less disposed to write letters to newspapers, we may assume a more discomforting picture still.

An indication of general public disquiet about government-controlled education both in Britain and elsewhere has been the rapid growth in home-schooling over the last ten years or so. Independent schools and nurseries have also seen a substantial increase in their numbers – especially those with a more 'relaxed' ethos. The particular relation to early years schooling of this tacit vote of no confidence seems confirmed by the immediate and significant growth in home-schoolers in Norway when, in 1997, the compulsory school age was reduced from seven to six years of age.

There are signs, we are happy to say, that at last the more extreme early-start policies are beginning to receive some more common-sense attention and modification. While the *Dispatches* programme was followed in its own country by an *even earlier* implementation of the National Curriculum, it has been heartening to note that David and Clare Mills, the programme makers, were invited to make a personal submission (in June 2000) to the British Government's Select Committee on Education and Employment. The contact was part of a general review of early years policy begun in July 1999, perhaps encouraged by the television programmes mentioned, perhaps even somewhat alarmed by them – and by the very real possibility that the Government was on the wrong track with its latest educational demands. Available to the select committee in its deliberations was an excellent annotated bibliography drawn up by the National Foundation for Educational Research, an independent organization supporting the work of local authorities and professionals in the field, of studies relating to school starting age, and the early years curriculum.[1] Also on the table was the publication *Early Learning Goals* drawn up by the Qualifications and Curriculum Authority for the current review. The select committee's deliberations led to recommendations which have been incorporated into Government early years policy under the new heading of *The Foundation Stage*.

'The Foundation Stage' refers to the education of children between 3 and 5, which is the period before schooling becomes compulsory in Britain and the National Curriculum key stage 1 begins. While from our own point of view the new guidelines for early years practitioners still beg many questions, they do nevertheless seem a real step in the right direction. In particular they show a welcome shift of emphasis away from intellectual expectations linked narrowly to literacy and numeracy to a more inclusive fostering of a child's developmental needs and potentials. They include the acknowledgement that a key way in which young children learn is through play. And they recognise the importance of early years practitioners working in partnership with parents and other adults sharing responsibility for particular children's welfare.

The change of both letter and spirit represented by the *Foundation Stage* guidelines is witnessed by the fact that a number of independent Steiner Waldorf kindergartens have felt able to apply for and receive government funding for their 4 year olds, knowing that they will thereby have to satisfy the Office for Standards in Education (Ofsted) that they are indeed doing the job 'by the book'. The inspections undertaken so far have led to generally very favourable reports, despite the fact that the Steiner kindergartens are clearly *not* preparing their 4 year olds to begin key stage 1 in the following year, but either to continue in Steiner

Waldorf education where they will receive their first formal introduction to literacy and numeracy when they are 6 or even 7, or simply to join mainstream education later with their own brand of preparation.

Perhaps the tide really is beginning to turn on these British shores. At the same time it seems to be swinging the other way in Norway, hitherto the outstanding 'late start' exemplar. The worrying factor in both cases is the degree to which any shift in educational policy may be motivated by political rather than truly educational concerns. The reason we are writing this book is that we believe childhood remains an unsafe condition to be in. The developed world as a whole represents a seething cauldron of conflicting interests where there is precious little opportunity for reflection on what is actually happening. Above all – and this lies at the heart of any question about education – there is precious little opportunity for unpressurized reflection on what it means to be human and to develop in a human way.

In the following chapter we shall consider what developmental issues are raised for all of us by the times we live in being 'out of joint'.

Some Findings of the High/Scope Project

The 68 children chosen for this research were all born in poverty. They were randomly assigned to one of the pre-school options, which they attended at the ages of 3 and 4. The following statistics were compiled 20 years later. The High/Scope scheme itself was initiated in 1967 and still continues today.

Mean number of adult arrests by age 23

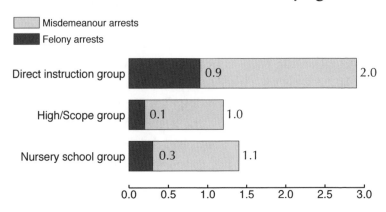

- ☐ Misdemeanour arrests
- ■ Felony arrests

Direct instruction group — 0.9 | 2.0

High/Scope group — 0.1 | 1.0

Nursery school group — 0.3 | 1.1

0.0　0.5　1.0　1.5　2.0　2.5　3.0

Three other curriculum effects

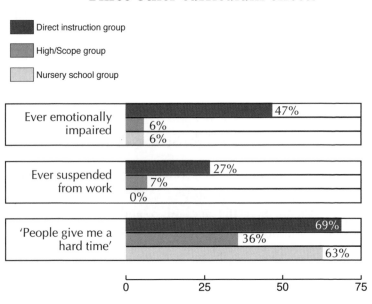

- ■ Direct instruction group
- ■ High/Scope group
- ☐ Nursery school group

Ever emotionally impaired
47%
6%
6%

Ever suspended from work
27%
7%
0%

'People give me a hard time'
69%
36%
63%

0　25　50　75

3. A Time of Miracles: The Child in Today's World

There are no achievements more fundamental and extraordinary than those belonging to the first chapter of life. Almost impossibly complex and subtle processes are re-enacted time and again, with such a disarming simplicity and such far-reaching consequences. Childhood is a time of miracles, and the whole of the rest of life is its outcome.

However, as a culture we have become impatient with ordinary miracles. We have been drawn instead to perform miracles of our own. And we've become good at it too: some truly extraordinary things *have* been achieved by human beings in our own times. It is hardly to be marvelled at that God and Nature have both lost their status in the face of the new 'superhumans'. Now even the status of 'human' is in question, as the possibilities of cloning become ever more of a reality. As a culture we have become obsessed with the possible. Like Tantalus, we believe in achieving what we think we want, and satisfying what we think are our needs seems perpetually within reach. So we go for it – on our own behalf, and on our children's behalf.

It is a sign of the times that in Britain we have a new educational hybrid, in which what were formerly called playgroups, nurseries, and kindergartens ('child gardens') are now amalgamated as so-called 'Early Years Settings'. It is a convenience, but also a potential epitaph. It signals a change of public consciousness in which childhood is being seen less as a time of natural and organic development, and more as a time for the application of generalized 'miracle grow' solutions. What was once a Secret Garden is now becoming a processing and packaging plant. Children who have barely got the feel of saying 'I', who have barely got the feel of their own bodies, who have barely begun to make sense of the world of their own senses – these same children are now being asked, even at the age of four, to engage in processes that are standard rather than individual, cerebrally rather than physically and imaginatively orientated, abstract rather than living and immediate. They are graded and labelled and, however subtly, priced... according to their value to a consumer society.

As we shall see in the following pages, *Ready to Learn* is not simply advocating a nostalgic 'back to nature' approach to childhood and early education. However, to the extent that human beings develop on this earth as living organisms, they are influenced, profoundly though not absolutely, by organic principles. Human development, like that of plants, is fundamentally rhythmic. As Ecclesiastes put it, there is a time for every purpose under heaven. There is a time to be born: for human beings, this is nine months after conception. Once upon a time, and not so very long ago either, we all still believed in other periods of gestation followed by a 'coming of age'. We sensed that children had a special coming of age at 7 – round about the time when they were changing their milk teeth. We sensed that a second coming of age occurred at 14 – around the time when most girls used to begin the menstruate, when apprenticeships were begun and when, in many cultures, rites of passage were (and sometimes still are) undergone by the flowering youth of the tribe. Then at the age of 21 came Independence

Day: the time, once symbolized by the right to vote, when society acknowledged that their young men and women had finally 'grown up' and attained both the stature and the responsibility befitting an adult.

It is both fascinating and frightening that all this now seems so much like a fairy tale. Not merely are the seven-year signposts no longer acknowledged by the adult world of today; they are apparently no longer acknowledged by developing children either. Teeth start to change at all sorts of times; periods begin at all sorts of times; teenagers overtake their parents in stature and, one might conclude, in their personal sense of stature – at all sorts of times... but almost always earlier than the ages of 7, 14, and 21. Biologists have a term for this: '*heterochrony*', which means 'differently synchronized'. The science of biology knows that all organic life, including the organic aspect of higher life forms, is essentially rhythmic and developmentally predictable. Heterochrony comes about when a particular rhythmic pattern loses its constancy. The observed fact that in just three generations, girls have come to start their periods over two years earlier is a striking instance of heterochrony within the human species (some of whom, it should be emphasized, have not undergone such acceleration.)

The physical manifestations of puberty are part of a powerful transformation that takes place right through the whole human psyche at this time. As the body ripens, so does the soul... or does it? Some girls start their periods at 10; but does this mean that they have the same inner maturity as a girl of 14? Or does it mean that the whole question of maturity is actually, for them, very confused? – another striking instance of heterochrony, this time within the interrelated rhythms of their own lives.

Human beings, let us reiterate, are simply not simple. They have physical bodies whose structures and processes are intricate, resilient, and efficient. Then they have an equally amazing inner life connoted by the word 'soul'; and thirdly, if we are to go along with the majority of human beings who have ever lived, there seems to be an element called 'spirit' which is also somehow involved in it. With all this developing simultaneously it is hardly surprising that it sometimes goes 'out of synch'.

To be human is to have a complex of development potentials whose unfolding is either more – or less – harmonious and successful. The fact that heterochronous discord is possible may in one case prove a catastrophe and in another case a miracle. The contention of this book is that we are in the middle of an increasing number of catastrophes, where human heterochronous development has become established as a conflict situation without a ready means of resolution. On the other hand, we are also living in the midst of miracles. A miracle is the transformation of one state of being by a principle belonging to a different state of being. All human development has, in this sense, the possibility of being miraculous, because whatever states we get ourselves into there is something else about us that can influence and potentially redeem that state. How many such miracles will *actually* be a part of our lives will depend, more than anything else, upon a quality we could simply call *vitality*.

In the next chapter we shall offer an evolutionary perspective on the question of vitality and adaptability, with special reference to the first years of life.

Main Points Again

- The first years of life are the most fundamental.
- Human capacities are extraordinary – but are we getting too clever for our own good?
- Human aspirations are increasingly centred around material success.
- The 'need to succeed' is driven ever deeper into the foundations of our lives.

- Children are increasingly 'forced' through their early years.
- Overlooking the organic aspect of human development has its price.
- Human life was once perceived to follow seven-year rhythms.
- Nowadays neither the idea nor the reality of such a seven-year rhythm seem much in evidence.
- A regular biological rhythm may appear to disappear when it becomes 'heterochronous'.
- Earlier beginning of menstruation as a twofold example of heterochrony.
- Heterochrony appears as a feature of human complexity.
- It leads to potential catastrophes, but also to potential miracles.

Practical Considerations

We need to distinguish between human developments and achievements that are motivated from within and those that reflect an outer influence. The influence of the outer world has become increasingly profound and disturbing in the lives of our children over recent decades. The fact that modern children may appear to rise to the occasion may indeed be true – but does that in itself mean that everything is all right?

4. An Evolutionary Perspective

There is an interesting evolutionary dimension to human development that points to a peculiar paradox in our biological nature. We would like to put this to you now as Nature's argument for 'holding back from the rat race'.

It is a well-established fact that one of the distinguishing characteristics of human beings is their uniquely prolonged childhood and adolescence. No other mammal has such a prolonged period of growth and development. What is more, this process – what biologists refer to as the lifeline or *life rhythm* – is not only longer than it should be for a typical mammal; it is also differently patterned.

Most large-brained mammals have a smooth continuous lifeline from birth to sexual maturity, at which point the animal has essentially reached its adult form. During this period of childhood the animals are capable of great learning. They are also playful – a fact which makes them so endearing to humans. However, as experience has shown with trained chimpanzees or dolphins, once they have reached adulthood, they can no longer be trained, they are no longer amusingly playful – in fact they become true to their native nature, which in the case of chimps can be aggressive and dangerous. The only animal that can apparently learn new tricks in adulthood is the elephant, who has seven changes of teeth.

The human child is born in an extraordinarily helpless state, with its limbs and body control almost totally ineffective, unable to maintain its own body warmth, and with a brain still in a highly unstructured state. In fact the human infant remains in what is, in effect, a foetal condition for months following the birth. The baby's brain, however, undergoes rapid and prolonged growth throughout the first year or so – and it is just as well that this happens. If we were born with the same brain/body weight ratio that a chimp or gorilla baby possesses, birth would be not just difficult, but impossible. Our heads would simply be too large to pass through the birth canal. Given what a tight squeeze the task already is, it is clear why the infant's brain cannot be any larger. The size of women's pelvis is determined by the mechanics of our upright position. Chimps, who are not upright walkers, have no such constraints on the size of their babies' heads.

Rapid brain growth means rapid learning capacity. The price we pay for having helpless, dependent infants for so long is amply rewarded by the large brain and large learning potential that accompanies it.

There is a biological law which states that the sooner an organism is exposed to the full force of selection processes in nature, the sooner that organism stops developing. So-called higher mammals have longer gestation periods, longer maturational lifelines, and require more parental support and protection. The most intelligent animals, with the richest, most complex social lives, have the longest periods of protected childhood.

However, humans not only have the longest period of childhood dependency; even after reaching sexual maturity we go on growing physically and maturing psychologically to beyond the age of 20, which in natural biological terms is almost half our life expectancy. Civilization has, of course, prolonged life expectancy to over 70 years, but our biological developmental period is still a significant fraction of this. It is this biologically determined, prolonged life of youth that gives us the possibility not only of being highly intelligent, creative, imaginative beings, but which also enables us to continue learning – lifelong. It is equally this very independence from the 'normal' compulsion of mammalian development that has given us the freedom to capitulate ourselves back into it. Because that is what accelerating our human development actually implies.

It may well allow us to become a breed of specialists such as no other mammal has ever yet been, but its ultimate direction is toward a Darwinian scrap-heap. Specialism is a short-term survival technique only. Even if we were to gain control over every biological principle on earth we would not thereby have gained the power to preserve our own humanity.

Main Points Again

- It is an evolutionary paradox that humans have an exceptionally retarded biological development.
- Childhood is Nature's gift for learning.
- Human infants retain a foetal capacity for rapid brain growth even after birth.
- 'Natural selection' actually works against higher development. Humans need protection from survival pressures for as long as possible if they are to develop to the full.
- Humans, uniquely, go on maturing even after sexual maturity.
- Our biological independence gives us the power to be either more or less human.

Practical Considerations

It is a limited and limiting view that children need 'hardening up' in order to survive in the 'real' world – an attitude passed especially along the male line. Might it be that the fact that boys are doing increasingly less well at school has to do with a hardening in their self-image which they adopt as a survival technique in the face of demands that seem too many and too soon?

5. Growing from the Roots: Getting the Early Stages Right

> 'Your flax soon kindles, soon is out again;
> My gold slow heats and long will hot remain.'
> John Webster, *The Duchess of Malfi*

A good gardener knows that 'hardening off' is a necessary part of transplanting a seedling to the outside world. He or she also knows what kind of care the seedling requires while it is still tender, when the right time for hardening off has arrived, and also knows the right way to do this. Let's now take an 'organic' overview of the child's garden, and further explore the question of what constitutes a healthy start to human life and learning.

The basic course (and we may after all still say this) of a normal and healthy child development traces, on the one hand, a process of growth and assimilation, and on the other a process of separation. The growth process unites the child with the world; the separation process involves the child becoming conscious of herself [2] and of the world as something separate from her. The two processes interact to change both self and world, and also the relationship between them.

The child's world and identity is determined initially by the mother and the immediate family and home environment. As the child grows physically in her first years she is also assimilating the whole of her surrounding world and incorporating it into herself very much as she does her material nourishment. She does this through a remarkable faculty of imitation, whereby she opens herself to the world through every one of her senses and accepts the impressions of the world directly into her being – like a wide open eye. Only gradually does she withdraw sufficiently from this sympathetic interaction to begin to do things on her own. Two signs that indicate this transition are when she says 'No' and when she says 'I', usually in the second to third year.

The second main stage of early learning that begins now is essentially about making relationships. These include different relationships between the *things* of the world and the *beings* of the world, and between all of these and the different personae of the child herself.

We can indicate the main features of the overlapping developmental phases of the young child as follows:

- **0-6 months**: establishing primary bodily functions, immune system, sleeping, feeding, and learning to recognize other people.
- **6-18 months**: stretching, sitting upright, grasping, exploring through movement, crawling.
- **18 months to 3 years**: walking, learning to talk.
- **3-6 years**: learning to think, learning to be with other people, learning to master the fine motor control of the limbs and fingers.

All of these activities are developing absolutely basic human faculties. Everything else – not least the so-called basic skills that formal education typically begins by addressing – follows from what is laid down here. Moreover, these first lessons in life are exceptionally demanding and sophisticated; and they require a quality and intensity of participation that only a youngster has the vitality and motivation to offer – and then only fully with the right kind of environment and support.

Little children love to chatter and run about and sing and dance and play games and have fantasies, because all of these experiences are not simply pleasurable but are also developing of human life skills. It may prove extremely exhausting for an adult to be involved in such activity – but *it is no less exhausting, and far less relevant, for a little child to be involved in adult activities* like sitting still for long periods and thinking about things. There is a genius to childhood that thrives on its own activity. Given a warm, loving human environment in which this is encouraged to take place, then a real Albert Einstein may develop out of it. As Einstein himself said: 'I have come to the conclusion that the gift of fantasy has meant more to me than any talent for abstract, positive thinking.'

Yet here we are, in a culture that seems determined to clip the wings of both genius and joy, when body and spirit are still so full of potential and at the same time so vulnerable. Some of the ways we do this are as follows:

- by asking children to do things before they are physiologically ready
- by flooding them with a welter of sense impressions they cannot properly process or digest
- by burdening them with emotional challenges they are totally unequipped to deal with
- by stunting the development of real mental capacity by premature intellectual learning
- by feeding them a diet of meaningless images when they seek real archetypal 'soul nourishment'
- by denying them the richness of human dialogue through offering the one-way monologue of the television screen
- by denying them an ordered and healthy environment, good nourishment, and the appropriate rhythms of life.

A plant that is starved or damaged in its roots can never really thrive, however well aspected its situation might otherwise be. On the other hand, a well-rooted plant that is in a generally favourable situation will continue to generate a fruitful energy through the whole of its life. So too with children: given a good start, and the right support through the continuation of their childhood, they will bear within them a fundamental capacity for regeneration. They will find themselves with a real potential to achieve miracles in the face of seemingly intractable problems; they will be natural survivors of mid-life crises, of the stresses of their careers and relationships, and of all that the slings and arrows that outrageous fortune have to throw at them. Above all, they will have, as their individual lives unfold, an inner relation to the common ground of all humanity – the people of which they are a part and the earth of which they are a part.

Main Points Again

- Child development involves both assimilation and separation.
- Through her faculty of imitation the child incorporates her impressions of the world directly into her being.
- The next phase, as the child begins to distinguish herself from her environment, is about making relationships.
- Early childhood has its own genius, which – with the best of intentions – we commonly thwart.
- A healthy beginning promises vitality for life.

Practical Considerations

Young children certainly need adults to participate actively in their lives. However, they are not themselves young adults, and we must be very careful not to treat them as such by making inappropriate intellectual, emotional, or practical demands of them.

6. Inheritance, Environment, and Individuality: The Human 'House'

In the previous chapter we presented an overview of how a child begins to relate to the word around her. Now we need to add a new element to the 'organic' metaphor as we come to consider more specifically what it means to grow up as a human being.

What does it mean to be born as a human being, not simply into the world but into a human body? We could borrow a comparison from another universal and typically traumatic experience, namely that of moving house. 'Moving house', of course, primarily means moving our self, or selves, between one house and another. Normally the process also includes taking with us much of what made our previous house 'home'. On arrival, if circumstances permit, our immediate task is to adapt the old to the new and, often more practically challenging, the new to the old. An aspect to be mentioned here is that most 'new' houses are actually acquired second-hand and bear the influence of their previous inhabitants, which also becomes relevant to the adaptation process. If all goes well, and the new house and its setting do quickly come to feel like home, then the rest of life can be got on with more happily and effectively than otherwise.

The human body is also a kind of house. The human being,

on being born, begins a process of moving into this house. Hitherto the infant's body has been the genetic property, so to speak, of the parents. This is one of the 'givens' of any new human life. Another given is the entirety of the environment that surrounds and impinges upon the newly housed infant, including the parents themselves, the other humans related to them, the actual brick and mortar house with its colours and gadgets and furnishings, the views through the windows and the reality represented by those views – and so on. All this is given as the child's world. The question is: Is it home?

This question would be pressing enough even if we took the view that heredity and environment were the only determining factors in human life. Many of us, however, have the instinctive conviction that a child brings something into life which is not simply the product of these other two factors, but a reality and influence in its own right. This 'something' represents what we would call the true spirit or being of the child. Where this being might actually come from, and what it might bring with it, are questions that will be answered quite differently; yet these differences of opinion need not, and generally do not, divide the recognition that children express, or certainly try to express, something uniquely individual and original. This 'something' will have everything to do with the sense of whether a child does or does not feel at home in its present life situation and, ultimately, with how we evaluate the meaning and potential of its unfolding activity in the world.

The points of the 'moving house' analogy might be summarized as follows:

- We all need a physical basis for our lives
- We inherit a physical body at birth in which we try to make ourselves comfortable, and which may be more or less easy to adapt and/or adapt to

- We are exposed to various environmental influences that affect this process, either positively or negatively
- We bring our own energy and creativity – our 'self-activity' – to meet what is given by our life situation
- Only when we have made ourselves feel basically at home do we readily turn our energy and creativity to other aspects of life.

As with many analogies this one only goes so far. One obvious difference between a body and a house is that the former is literally a 'living' space, and is determined by physiological as well as simply physical considerations. Physiological processes – life processes – take place in time; and they take place in their own time. Moving into a body is certainly not an overnight affair, and any attempt to hurry it will have definite consequences, both for the body itself and its inhabitant. It is also the case that physiological processes are subject to environmental influence in a different way from physical conditions, being essentially far more sensitive. This is especially the case in early life, where the child's body is still like a house with no curtains.

Then there is the special significance of the parental influence, which both suffuses the body as inherited at birth and represents the most dominant presence in the child's immediate environment. When we move house in the ordinary sense we don't normally expect to find the previous occupants still living in it, nor semi-detatchedly on either side of it. Yet this is how things generally go with the birth-house, and on the whole we must be extremely grateful for it too, given that a child is after all a child. Nevertheless, there is an inherent possibility in this situation that the parental influence may prove inhibiting as well as encouraging, making it more difficult than it should be for the child to incorporate her own individuality into the foundations of her own future life.

The next stage of our discussion will focus more closely on the crucial significance of the child's 'self-activity' – with some wonderful illustrations of this process from children's drawings.

Main Points Again

- Being born may appear like moving into a new house.
- How does the child feel at home with her genetic inheritance and her new environment?
- This is a question concerning the true individuality of the child.
- Inhabiting a body takes its own time.
- Parental influence may help or hinder the child's 'self-activity'.

Practical Considerations

'Doesn't he look like his dad?' Perhaps, but his deepest aim will be to look, and be, himself.

7. Moving into the Body: The Child's Picture

New-born children tell us about themselves through their movements and cries. To begin with these expressions are reflexive and involuntary, and they indicate how awake the baby is, and how comfortable and content. Within hours of being born the child is active, seeking contact, informing us of her needs. Over the first few months the movements and vocal utterances become more specific, announcing moments of self-discovery and deliberate communications with the outside world. One lovely highlight of this period is the child's first smile.

By about five months the infant has achieved a truly Olympian feat, never again to be repeated within such a time-scale: she has literally doubled her birth weight! The next doubling will be attained when she is around two years old, then when she is eight, and lastly when she is sixteen. The first great aim of life is to grow. Nothing is more important to the infant than eating and sleeping – both essential to healthy growth. Whatever form of communications the child may be using in these first months will be directed instinctively to this end.

A second human compulsion begins to emerge out of the first – *the urge to stand up*. Through a gradually unfolding process, which begins with the head, moves down to the trunk, and finally penetrates the lower limbs, the child determinedly struggles against the forces of gravity toward that wonderful moment when she takes her own first step. Although this has the appearance of being a compulsive human activity it is actually not instinctive, but depends on the child being raised in a human environment. The urge to stretch, stand, and walk is a primary expression of what we are calling the child's self-activity, and it is qualitatively different from the instinct which drives young calves or foals, for example, to stagger to their feet.

The human being expresses a need to reach out to meet the world. Initially this is through the senses – the first stretching movements have to do with turning and lifting that heavy head to get a better view. Soon this is followed by an urge to reach out into that view. This proceeds through the various stages of sitting and crawling to the gravity-defying act of balancing on feet that are still soft and rounded. Driven by curiosity, the process of uprightness requires the sympathetic support and encouragement of those around the child, though not in the form of artificial aids which substitute for the child's own activity.

Just as the child's own impulse to re-orientate herself is not purely instinctive, neither is her imitation of other humans purely an outer emulation. It is not the outer bio-mechanics of walking that she imitates, but the inner act of equilibrium and intentional mobility. Her increasing responsiveness to her environment is reflected in the complex changes in her movement patterns, and speech, as the initial growth phase begins to slow down.

Somewhere between 18 months and two years the child adds a new form of expression to her repertoire. Her clutching hand gets hold of a pencil or crayon – and whether on paper, table, or wall she begins to translate her movements into form. After a while she begins to notice these 'special effects' and is further encouraged to make more of them. In this first phase of scribbling the child is not attempting to copy or represent anything objectively 'out there'. The drawing is simply a means of reinforcing what we may call movement-perception and movement-memory. Having said this, the scribblings of infants show universal motifs, and clearly have an objective correlation to *something*.

Perhaps the most obvious common denominator of these movement-drawings is that they are rhythmic and repetitive. So too are life and growth processes, and also processes of perception and consciousness. The proposal we want to make here is that *there is indeed a direct link between what young children draw and the life processes going on inside them*. The motifs in the drawings are not merely universal in themselves; they also follow a typical progression. While not every child demonstrates the sequence with equal clarity, the pattern is nevertheless too consistent to be overlooked. We cannot overlook the fact that the progression in children's drawings follows, and indeed mirrors, a parallel progression in their general development. We find ourselves looking at an exhibition of *inner developmental pictures*, expressed externally.

The first stage of scribbling is reminiscent of an unhinged pendulum or a whirligig whose somewhat chaotic path is traced on and off the paper in both a horizontal and vertical plane. Initially appearing and disappearing like the signature of a passing discarnate entity, these scrawls begin to intensify as time goes on – as does the child's absorption in them. The whirligig begins to dominate, swirling round and round itself like a swarm of bees around its queen:

Boy
1 year 11 months

As the bee swarm comes to settle around its centre, so too does the child's whirl. The circling develops a more deeply inscribed little oscillation at its heart that brings it to rest:

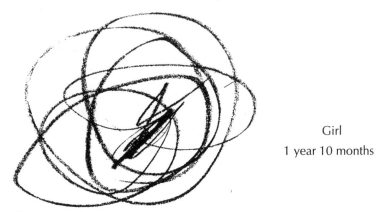

Girl
1 year 10 months

A circling that moves regularly toward its centre becomes a spiral, which is the next transformation of the whirligig motif in children's drawings. The in-winding spiral (young children always seem to draw spirals that wind inwards) is classically a symbol of concentration and purpose. From reflexive to intentional movement, and from peripheral sensation to centred consciousness, children follow a spiral journey whose first chapter takes normally some three years to conclude.

The conclusion takes us beyond the spiral itself, which is essentially an open form, into the realm of the closed circle. What an effort the child puts into its creation, and what a triumph its achievement represents! Once the single circle has been established the spiral is further transformed into a nest of circles within circles, and then simplified to a circle with a single point at its centre.

This is a hugely significant moment. It is now that we may feel the child to be 'moved in' and at home. It is also now that we may expect to hear the child speak meaningfully in the first person as 'I'.[3] This phase may be marked by the closing of the fontanelles – the soft spaces between the bones of a young child's head.

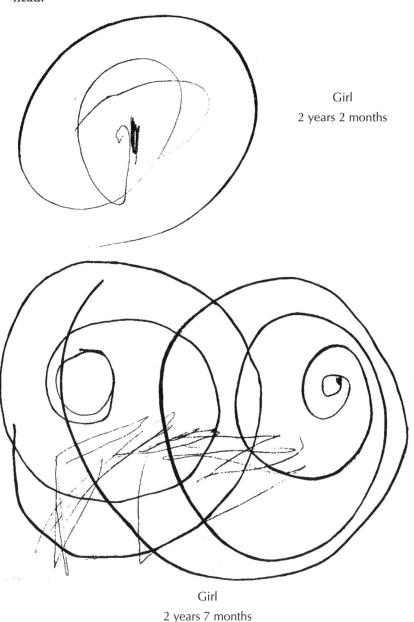

Girl
2 years 2 months

Girl
2 years 7 months

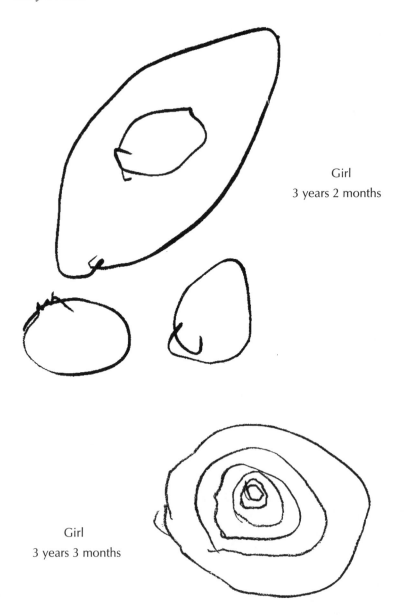

Girl
3 years 2 months

Girl
3 years 3 months

The route to this crucial nodal point in development is mapped through another motif in the drawing process. This is the metamorphosis of the pendulum movement we noted earlier. In its original manifestation the swinging of the crayon to and fro shows no particular orientation to the horizontal and vertical. Gradually, however, it is these two directions which predominate; and out of the special relation between them emerges the figure of the cross. This too is an image of centredness, and it is also an image of balance. The more openly we look at children's cross drawings the more readily we may see them as proto-images of the upright human being, still in a 'scarecrow' condition but recognizable nevertheless.

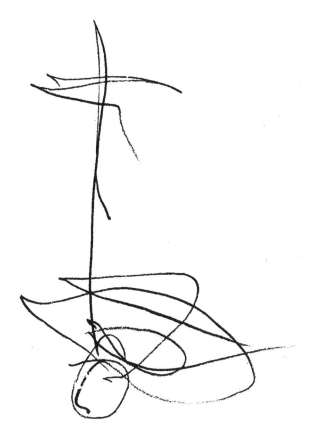

Boy
1 year 9 months

Girl
2 years 1 month

The parallel developments of the circle and cross culminate with them combining together in a new image. The cross enters and centres the circle.

What happens next? The child, having established her own presence and sense of security within her new 'house' and its setting, begins to explore further. The following illustrations express a radial expansion from the centre point, first into the inner space of the circle and then beyond its boundary. All this corresponds with the child's growing ability to associate, identify, and relate to the content of her perceptions in ordinary life:

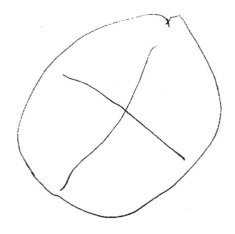

Boy
3 years 7 months

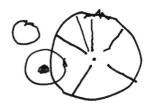

Girl
3 years 4 months

Boy
3 years 2 months

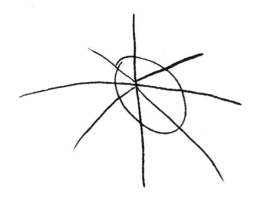

Boy
4 years 5 months

Only as the child approaches her fifth year does she begin to establish a representational rather than symbolic drawing process. A final geometric motif appears as a marker for this transition. Having mastered circular and cross (together with rectangular and ladder) forms, the child now focuses more deliberate attention on the diagonal. The St Andrew's cross appears superimposed on the earlier St George's cross, and finally the different spatial directions coalesce into the triangle.

Behind the scenes of this achievement stands the biological fact that human beings are organized with twin hemispheres to their brains, whose functions are destined to include the co-ordination of their diagonally opposite body movements. This function is not established all at once. Before it is fully operative, normally around 6 or 7 years of age, a right-handed child will pick up a crayon lying to the left of her with her left hand – then pass it to her right. She balks at crossing her 'midline barrier', as it is called.

Only when the child is aware of the different directions of space in her own physiology can she begin to express them outwardly. Once she does have this possibility, however, the conscious attempt to draw objectively becomes part of her integration into the outer world. Doing a drawing becomes something like taking a walk down the garden path. What makes these drawings so wonderful to us is that they transport us into a garden world, where the outer forms, more or less recognizable and nameable in themselves, are simply bursting with inner life and colour. The five-year-old's drawings are representations, not of the objective world as such, but of her imagination of the world, where inner and outer realities are equally real and valid. At this stage a crucial element of the child's inner reality is still the developing landscape of the body and its processes. In the ideal biography the child will explore this garden world until she knows it inside out; only then will she open the gate and walk on.

Main Points Again

- The infant's reflexive activity slowly becomes more focused.
- The infant's first aim is to grow.
- Then she struggles to imitate the uprightness of her human family.
- Curiosity is the motive force in early movement.
- The child learns to walk through linking her own self-activity with the self-activity of others.
- As her movements become more purposeful this becomes reflected in her early drawings.
- The child's first drawings are not representations of outer things but expressions of vital, rhythmic movements and inner life processes. They typically evolve through the following motifs:
    - Early swirlings...
    - Beginnings of centredness
    - The spiral
    - The closed circle
    - Circles within circles, then the circle with its centre point
    - The 'pendulum'
    - The cross and the 'scarecrow'
    - The cross within the circle...
    - ...and going beyond the circle
    - The triangle, coupled with the establishing of laterality.
- Even outer representations are still pictures of the young child's inner world.

Practical Considerations

Children begin drawing literally out of themselves. They need plenty of opportunity for this form of self-exploration and development – but not to be made overly conscious of what they are drawing. If the child wants to talk about a drawing, that's fine – but let the child be the initiator.

8. Making Sense of the World

In the previous chapter we explored how the child moves into her own body as the precursor to stepping fully out into the world. Now we will consider how the youngster takes the world into herself.

The picture of a little baby suckling milk tells us a great deal about how, in a more general sense, she takes in the world around her. Especially at this early stage the process of making sense of the world is actually very closely akin to the process of assimilating and digesting nourishment. The healthy child is also a hungry child: firstly for her milk and then, with increasing focus, for sense impressions.

It is generally agreed nowadays that the healthiest physical nourishment for human infants is human milk. It is also generally accepted that, for emotional as well as physical reasons, it is preferable when possible for the child to be breast- rather than bottle-fed.[4] It is also becoming more commonly accepted that, apart from the possible remoteness of medical help, the ideal place for a child to be born and first to meet the world is at home. And we all agree that the ideal first company for a baby is human beings, above all the mother.

Why is breast milk so special? Because, at least when the mother is healthy, it contains exactly the right balance of nutrients (and this is something which adjusts itself naturally according to need) in a form which has effectively been pre-digested and 'humanized' by the mother. As regards the activity of breast-feeding, it is clearly a much more intimate interchange than bottle-feeding, and it softens the transition from womb to world. The same consideration applies to the wider environment of early life: the more 'maternal' it feels, the more directly it will nourish both mother and child. A further significant feature of breast-feeding is that it is an active process, in which the baby is 'taking on' the world rather than simply passively receiving it.

The baby needs and expects its food to be good. With its whole being it instinctively roots for this goodness, open-mouthed and hungry. However, it has little power to deal with what is not good for it. There is, to be sure, a basic reflex reaction to what is perceived as not good, where the baby rejects the intrusive substance totally. However, once a substance does get past the outer defences and into the system, the infant's metabolism is very much at its mercy. At this stage more than any other the maxim 'You are what you eat' applies. The ability to transform substance, taking what is needed from it without being overwhelmed by it, is something that has to be developed. This takes both time and the careful provision of a menu which is both healthy and appetizing.

All that has been said about physical nourishment applies to everything else that the child takes in from the world via the gateway of her senses. Here too the infant both needs and expects goodness, reaching out and drawing in whatever impinges upon her awareness just as it does her mother's milk. To say that the growing child is affected by her environment is rather an understatement: she is affected by the *impressions* of the world as deeply as she is affected by the *substance* of the world. Sudden sounds or bright lights invade the child's inner sanctuary and write themselves directly upon its walls. And these 'walls' are so soft and receptive that the impressions are absorbed and incorporated right into them.

We see a related though far less profound instance of this

process when we look at the face of an adult. Impressions of the world get written, perhaps only momentarily, into the facial expression. The stronger the impressions, and the more they are repeated, the more they linger in the physiognomy. They may even appear as permanent features. The farm worker's or coal miner's faces are obvious examples. But the face of a person who has lived a painful, embittered life is equally marked.

The baby's body is more open than an adult face, more responsive and impressionable – like an open eye that only closes when the baby sleeps. However, while the physical eye initially translates outer reality into *mental* images, the impressions received through the baby's sense organization are translated more directly into life processes, which in turn translate themselves, at this stage of child development, into *physical* forms. If this were immediately and outwardly obvious there would no doubt be a huge change in the way we bring up children. Sadly, however, what the child experiences in early life may take years to manifest.

It is true that an infant needs stimulus in its life right from the beginning. Birth itself is, of course, about as big as stimulus gets. However, once the life processes have been shocked into the activity appropriate to living outside the womb (and even this doesn't have to be as shocking as it often is) the child needs protection more than exposure. As a bird changes egg for nest so the child should feel 'wrapped up' in her world, not only in her cot but in the whole way her environment is softened, muted and kept warm.

The majority of parents have an instinctive sense of this need, which helps them get the first steps right. However, the pressures of their own life-styles and the pressures of contemporary expectations start to work against what they might feel in their heart to be right. It is no longer assumed that mothers have a natural duty to sacrifice their other options by extending total involvement with child-rearing beyond gestation itself, let alone beyond weaning. And there are very good reasons why this should not be assumed.

Rather more questionable, however, is the current implication that raising a child beyond the first weeks or months under a 'Madonna's cloak' is both outmoded and unduly precious. Nevertheless, it is accepted current practice to integrate a baby quickly into the prevalent life-style, involving much moving in and out of the home environment, the unpredictable appearing and disappearing of familiar faces, and continued exposure to the rapid-fire impressions of modern technology. The same impulse lies behind the whole drive toward early education. It is an impulse that in our view is misguided in its assumptions, and is not helping our children to make sense of their world.

Making sense of the world begins with the sense of touch. Perhaps we can still remember just how sensitive we were as children to the 'feel' of things. Touching was, and is, a real communion. We experience this especially when we touch the skin of another person. We also respond to the 'living' feel of other materials. Infants deprived of physical intimacy fail to thrive. Those new-born children who have to spend time in incubators do better being laid on sheepskin than on synthetic materials. It makes a difference what we clothe or wrap our children in, and what we give them to suck and hold.

It also makes a difference whether things stay in the same place and happen at the same time in a child's world. Children up to about their third year only believe what they see. If it isn't there it isn't real. A continuous sense of reality is developed through experiences being repeated. The more predictable these repetitions become, the more strongly they embed themselves into the child's consciousness. All of this points to the child's need for rhythm, repetition, and continuity in the stream of its early impressions.

How does an infant move? The fact is, she is compulsively drawn to imitate the movements going on around her. If she were raised by robots she would move like a robot, just as if she were raised by wolves she would move like a wolf. At the same time she is inwardly predisposed to find more meaning in living than mechanical movements, and most meaning of all in human movements. Given that there are so many non-human movements in the modern world it is essential that we compensate for this in the way we ourselves move in children's presence.

And so with the sensations of warmth or cold, the smells and tastes, the sight and sounds: it is their warmth and humanity that the child is really interested in. This is what will lead her willingly and actively through an otherwise meaningless maze of sense perceptions toward the ability to make sense of the world through language and thought.

Healthy development involves continually creating a balance between extremes. A middle way needs to be found between over-stimulation and under-stimulation of growing children. They benefit from a child-friendly environment and from being protected but not smothered by tender loving care. If possible they should be nourished by their mother's milk but then weaned from it as soon as they are ready to 'humanize' their food themselves.

To conclude this chapter, we might recall the fact we discussed earlier, that of all creatures on earth the human being takes the longest to mature and to achieve the possibility of real independence. When we get there, however, we are by far the most independent and adaptable of all creatures. Our flexibility, adaptability, and freedom depend on possibilities developing which can only unfold in the special situation of a semi-protected environment that allows faculties to develop and integrate themselves into the world slowly, broadly, and deeply. A premature advancement out of this special condition may well lead to survival and an apparently successful adaptation to a particular life situation, but this may nevertheless be a more limited and less fulfilling achievement than it might have been.

Of course, differing degrees of outer disruption or even chaos are inevitably part of many peoples' lives. While the effect of this on young children should not be understated, the crucial factor in all childcare is the continuity and quality of love and responsibility in the child's human environment.

Main Points Again

- The child is nourished through the senses as well as through the milk.
- The maternal quality in the child's environment makes her feel 'at home'.
- The child's environment, as nourishment, needs to make a 'good' impression.
- Sense impressions work on in the inner life processes, moulding the physical body.
- The child needs a balance of stimulation and protection.
- There are dangers to integrating infants too soon into modern life-styles.
- Sense of touch gives first impressions of the world.
- A child's security depends on rhythm and continuity.
- We need to be aware of what movements a child experiences around her.
- The child seeks human meaning in what she perceives.
- Balance is all-important.
- Human beings have a naturally prolonged childhood for good reason.

Practical Considerations

The effects of diet in infancy have received considerable study over recent decades, but the influence of early sense impressions, which is no less significant, is far less centred in common awareness. This is an area where parents can promote or hinder their child's well-being – through the quality of personal time they spend with their children, the toys they give them, the exposure to or protection from the hurricane of electronic sounds and images and other lifeless 'life-forms' that are sweeping through the world.

9. Making Maps: The Development of Cognition

There is a wonderful story that highlights an important truth about maps. A Chinese emperor was concerned that he should have accurate maps of his entire kingdom, so that he could rule better. Each time his cartographers returned to show him maps, he would study areas he knew well to test their accuracy. He first noticed that the mountain in fact had two peaks and not only the one depicted on the map. Later he noticed that close by a ford in a certain river he knew, there stood an old willow tree, not represented on the map. He complained that the layout of his palaces and their stables was not accurate, and even that a hermit sitting in a cave was absent. Each map the cartographer made to meet his requirements was bigger to show more detail. In the end the Emperor was still not satisfied with a map, whose borders reached those of the kingdom itself. However large or detailed your map, it is no substitute for the real thing, and it can't be walked through.

In addition to what cartographers may do, we also make maps in our minds through a process that has come to be called 'mental mapping'. These maps are mental representations 'in here' of what we experience 'out there', and they have essentially the same function as the cartographer's map, namely to assist in our orientation and to categorize information using symbols. They also function as a form of memory. The easiest mental maps to describe are those in which we recall the layout of our house, our path to school, the surroundings we're familiar with. These are based on our experience of moving around these spaces. They record what we have noticed and find important in our environment. However, what constitutes the 'out there' that we represent 'in here' is not always as obvious.

In the young child's development the process of mental map making is a vital one and begins very early. This is related to the growth in the brain of certain nerve cells called neurons which, in growing, send out tentacle-like extensions called axons which meet and link up with the axons of other neurons. Each neuron can have many hundreds of axons and the total number of connections between all the neurons in the cortex of the brain can be calculated in astronomical numbers. The combinations of connections are practically infinite. The vast number of inter-linked networks provides a neural basis for a vast number of mental mapping operations. This is obviously an over-simplification, but it provides us with all we need to know at this stage to account for the physiological basis of mental mapping. The more important point is what these maps *represent*, and how they serve the child.

As we have seen, the young child is flooded with sense impressions, many of them new. She does not yet possess the capacity to understand them, or indeed to filter out those she cannot deal with. As a result these impressions flow largely unmediated by cognitive processes straight into the life processes and work there to influence the shaping and forming of the organ-building activity, which is intensive at this early stage of life. One example we discuss in the chapter on language is the child's imitation of perceived speech sounds, which help shape the speech organs themselves. Another example is the fine structuring of the brain.

However, the infant is not passive. She possesses a number of important predispositions, the primary one being the self-activity we call *focus of attention*. The child is not *passively* open to the world but, within the flood of her impressions, is actively seeking contact and directing her attention to her rapidly expanding environment. Starting with the mother or mother figure, the child soon shows interest in other people and objects around her. There are reflexes which are certainly genetically predetermined, but this active interest is not merely a physical compulsion. Any parent can confirm the experience of looking at their baby and knowing with certainty that there is *someone* there. This someone is a spiritual being with a powerful drive to develop the wherewithal to experience the world and express itself. As a spiritual being, the child has an affinity with *being* in the world around her.

We can see here a two-way process in which sense impressions flow into the child from the environment and are met with the activity of the child herself, radiating as it were from within. The being of the young child at this stage is dominated by a powerful existential hunger for experience and the satisfaction of primary needs. Anything that disrupts or hinders this, such as belly hunger, the discomfort of nappy rash, or lack of attention, produces a protest that is impossible to ignore. Mothers have to learn quickly to recognize what their children need. If an adult were to protest with such vigour the results would probably be terrifying, so powerful is the young child's frustrated will. When the child sleeps, she is equally active – only this activity is directed inward to digesting and assimilating the nourishment and sense impressions she has received.

As a spiritual being herself the child is drawn to that which has *being* in her environment. How does she know what has being? Other human beings announce themselves through their own activity, but significantly the child's attention is drawn to what other people find important. They imitate our interest in what is around us. That means they notice what we notice, they care for what we care for. An environment which people deeply care for is therefore far more interesting, and is thus far more nourishing for an infant or young child.

All this self-directed activity needs to be structured and ordered, and an infant spends huge amounts of energy processing its experiences and learning how to manage its own rapidly growing bodily instrument. Every sense impression has to be decoded, recognized, and related to other sense impressions in order that a perception can occur. Seeing and hearing are not simply open windows through which sounds and sight enter into the cinema of the mind. These are much more active processes, since the primary sensory information itself is broken down in the act of perception into a range of different components that are relayed by different sensors. In the eye, for example, some sensory cells are sensitive to specific colours, others to vertical lines within our field of vision, and other still relate to the brightness factor. These partial impressions have to be re-integrated before a comprehensible picture of what the child is looking at can be formed in the 'mind's eye'. In order to grasp the three-dimensionality of an object, several 'views' have to be compared before the sense of the object's solidity or depth can be experienced. This too involves a kind of mapping.

Overload

It has been observed that over the past 20 years there has been an average of 1 per cent reduction in the sensory sensitivity of the human mind, with a corresponding loss of ability to receive information about the world. That means the maps 'in here' have 20 per cent less detail than they recently had, which is a massive loss of consciousness. Children could, for example, differentiate 360 shades of red; now, only a generation later, that number has been reduced to around 130 shades. One could say, 'well, 130 is still a lot'. But if we translate that into the full range of sense perceptions, the significance of this loss should stagger us. If somebody forced all children to wear special glasses which cut out 20 per cent of what they could see, there would be loud protest against this forced disempowerment of our most important citizens!

Joseph Chilton Pearce, a highly respected researcher into human intelligence and learning, highlights a further aspect of this problem. The kind of stimulus necessary to make an impression on the modern child's mind, now needs to be more intense. We need 'highly concentrated bursts of over-stimulation. That is, the only signals they're really bringing in from their environment are those bursts of stimuli that are highly charged. If it's sound it must be a loud sound. If it's visual, it must be intense. Subtleties cannot catch their attention because they are not sensitive to their environment.'[5] Overload leads to less detailed maps, hastily constructed, less adequately integrated, and poorly encoded memories that can only take account of ever larger, stronger, brighter, louder input.

Given the kind of world in which we live, children will be bombarded by a flood of sense impressions, many in the form of images that seek to capture the mind by imprinting their message. The kind of sensory apparatus we have inherited has evolved over millions of years to meet quite different needs in totally different environments. In a crowded shopping mall our natural capacities are all but overwhelmed, which is why even adults find it tiring! We have far outstripped the evolutionary heritage we carry around in our genes. That, however, is just how it is. We have to *learn* to adapt, as opposed to waiting for nature to adapt our physical organs for us.

If we can't adapt our cognitive strategies by superimposing higher levels of meaning and selection, then we will flounder and be at the mercy of the flood of impulses. We see the effects of this in hyperactive children who are easily bored and who continuously appear to need new stimuli. The other extreme is withdrawal, a shutting down to all but a few stimuli, leading to lack of interest, apathy, and a preoccupation with what is going on, not in the world but internally.

We can be proactive by acknowledging the situation, rather than ignoring it or saying, 'well, the children will just have to manage'. We can take the initiative in several ways. First, we can seek to limit the flood of rapidly changing sense impressions that the young child is as yet unable to process or digest – for example, by preventing, or severely limiting, very young children's access to television. We can also make sure that children have enough time to develop the capacities they need to deal with the sense impressions they will inevitably have to deal with.

We realize that this is no easy challenge for the modern parent, though younger children are more easily engaged in other activities than older children. Young children are happiest when doing what Mummy or Daddy is doing. Literally doing real domestic tasks is not easy to arrange, but children can be engaged with a few toys doing *their* washing up, cooking *their* dinner, or ironing *their* clothes. And wherever possible it will be of untold benefit to enable children to experience as wide a range of natural sense experiences as possible, whether out in the countryside, in the garden, or in the materials of the play basket.

Because of the absolute importance to all further learning of the child's first mental picturing, we will follow this chapter with a more detailed look at specific aspects of children's 'early maps'.

Main Points Again

- From early in the womb, right up until well after school age (authorities differ as to how long this process continues, some even suggesting well into adulthood), the child is busy constructing and fine tuning the brain, our central organ of consciousness.

- We construct 'in here' in our minds a picture of ourselves and how we perceive the world.
- The quality of sense impressions a child experiences greatly influences this process.
- The way we understand the world and relate to it is strongly formed by our early, primary sense impressions, especially their coherence.
- Sensory overload is a major problem in the development of a coherent picture of the world, one the child can relate to.

10. Activity Maps

The child lives in two environments that she initially cannot distinguish. The world as presented through the senses constitutes one of these worlds, and the 'world' of the child's own organism and later mind, the '*in here*' world, is the other. The very young child needs to map the 'in here' world in a very specific way if she is to have control over her movements – and the child *wants* to control her ability to take hold of the world and engage with it. Initially the impulse to move and the child's intentions are not co-ordinated. But the child wants to impose her intentions on the activity of movement which in itself has no specific direction but is best described as a centrifugal force radiating from the child into the world.

An experiment by the child psychologist Ester Thelen makes this point clear. Thelen set out to observe how children learn to co-ordinate their hands, and in particular to observe the mental mapping process it involves. Children were placed in a high-chair (apparently standard equipment in child psychology labs as well as in domestic settings), and an object, such as a cup of juice, was placed in front of them. The child was suitably wired up so that the researchers could monitor the brain functions that accompanied the activity. Thelen observed how the children initially make a series of undirected arm movements, constrained only by the anatomy of the arm, which of course favours grasping of objects in front of the body at chest height. With each movement, groups of neurons would become active – this is evocatively termed *firing* in the neurology field because the activity lights them up on the monitor. Each time the child manages, initially more by chance than direction, to grab hold of the cup she becomes more proficient at the task, and the neural networks that reflect the right combination of movements to achieve the desired results are repeatedly fired. This repetition (which is never an exactly identical pathway but rather a similar and overlapping pattern) reinforces the network.[6]

This process reveals a number of highly interesting aspects. First, the child's activity is stimulated by an impulse or urge to grab the cup in the first place. One can ask where this comes from. The neurologist might explain that the activity was prompted by a genetically predetermined reflex or stimulus, in both the motive and the manner of the movements. There is, to be sure, an inborn 'feed me' impulse at work; there is also an inherent capability in the construction of the human hand and arm which is 'set' for this kind of movement. But one only has to observe how the child actually carries out such activity to experience her *active presence* in the process. This is what we are calling the child's self-activity, with the suggestion that it represents, here in a powerful and primary form, a truly spiritual impulse to find self-realization through life experience.

So what is it that stimulates the reinforcement of the appropriate neural pathways? In fact it is the joy the child has in the fulfilment of her intention, her success in being able to grasp the cup, and no doubt her enjoyment of the recognition provided by the mother who witnesses the deed. All these add up to the presence of a powerful emotional factor in the equation. We know that such neural pathways are literally reinforced by the growth of a sheath of fatty protein called myelin around the nerve fibres most activated – that is, most often selected. Other, less-used pathways degrade. This means that an emotional reaction helps to fix the physical structure of the neural networks that map the movement needed to grasp a cup. Every learned movement skill has to be established in this way.

These kind of maps (and we must remember that we have no consciousness of their formation or activity) form the substantial basis for the child's volitional activity. One could say that the child is in a permanent state of movement. Mostly it is internal but it also manifests in the outer movement of the eyes, hands, and so on, and this movement is directed by the child's unconscious will. The sight of the cup directs the flow of this activity toward the cup, one could say, with all systems firing. There is no reflection and the feeling element is entirely bound up with the activity. Only much later can reflective thought, as it were, slip between feeling and will activity, separate it out, and become conscious of the experience.

Main Points Again

- Joy in movement has healthy consequences for the body as well as the soul.

- The intellect should not be over-stimulated before the child has had time to build a basis of primary movement-imbued experience.

11. Memory Maps

We construct, in milliseconds and deep below the threshold of consciousness, a map of the object in front of us. When the object is familiar, which means we have mapped similar objects before, the maps we produce can begin to be generalized. Our awareness of this is what we call a concept. The greater the perceived detail, intensity, and clarity of the sense perceptions, the more comprehensive the concept. The child's activity of comparing maps to form concepts grows slowly and (unless other factors intervene) surely out of the foundation of her activity maps.

Once the child can move her head and focus the eyes, several perspectives are available. Once the child can move around the room, wholly new spaces are revealed to be discovered and mapped. Once she can run outside, the horizons rapidly expand. Throughout all this process of discovery the child increasingly needs to relate here to there, to know how to get from *here to there* and back. Only gradually is it possible to recognize that the way back is the same one as the journey there. Naturally it looks different. Each journey made is punctuated by encounters that make the journey literally memorable.

Here is a big pot of flowers that needs watering; there is mummy's wheelbarrow which I like to sit in, but it's a bit wobbly when we drive it; and this is where I fell and bumped my knee, but we kissed it better and it's all right now.

Each noticed object has its significance, has a story to tell, evokes a memory. Revisiting a place revives those memories and experiences, and enhances them with meaning. Indeed this is how memory arises. In mapping our experiences in association with the place and situation in which they occurred, we construct not only a spatial map but a temporal one too.

The earliest forms of memory are in fact locational and situational. When a familiar object appears it awakens the impulse of the activities associated with it. Children learn things in sequences of activities, *this happens, then that happens, and then we can do that.* When the objects representing a sequence of activities or experiences are not present, it is much harder for the child to recall them. Experience shows, however, that children of two to three years old already need very little stimulus to recall situations. It appears as if Tom has suddenly remembered that there are ice-lollies in the fridge which are not visible, but close observation shows that some sense-perceptible clue will have triggered the memory. It may be as obvious as the sight of the fridge, but it may be as subtle as seeing a stick shaped like a lolly stick or even hearing mention of a word that sounds like lolly (remembered delight)!

When children begin to be able to do this they are entering a new phase of representation. Now they are able to trigger memories, think of things, or start activities prompted by images that represent the thing or concept. Initially and for a long time, this form of representation remains rich in associations of tangible, real experience. The images represent a very broad and flexible range of experience. In this phase something wonderful happens.

Let us take an everyday example, that of a four year old playing at making and serving tea. The living experience of tea-making is so strong that once the topic has arisen, by association or adult suggestion, any old object will do to act out the drinking of tea, and visitors may be offered a shell or a block of wood with the explanation that it is a cup of tea. One may not be given much time to drink as the shell is unceremoniously taken back and the action repeated. In this case the *activity* of pouring and offering the tea is what is important. We discuss the development of play through various stages in Chapter 15 on 'Child's Play'. For now we wish to focus on aspects of representation.

We therefore have two aspects of this stage of representation. In the first the child sees a bottle of apple juice and wants to have a drink. In the other, the activity of pouring and drinking the juice is applied to whatever comes to hand. In both cases a sense perception or a suggestion stimulates the activity. In both cases the representation is very much of picture character. Memory can retain pictures far more readily (and this goes for adults too) than abstract symbols for the obvious reason that they evoke more levels of experience and constitute an organic whole. It is easier to recall a sequence of pictures that tell a story and are full of feelings, than it is a list of telephone numbers.

If an experience is accompanied or clothed by a sense of wonder, by enthusiasm, by joy and love, these feelings will colour the memory. Each time this memory is recalled, something of the underlying emotional intensity is re-perceived. Often such emotional content remains below the threshold of full consciousness and manifests as a feeling that may pervade our mood and thus influence our attitudes. Since young children have a powerful innate sense of empathy, the feelings of wonder, for example, that an adult experiences with the child will be imitated and reinforced. This is the basis for establishing deep-seated moral sensibilities in children because children also want to learn what the right feelings are in a given situation.

Each time we recall and reflect on our experiences, we add another dimension of significance and meaning to the maps. Each time we encounter similar experiences we are able to expand

and, to mix metaphors, 'deepen' our maps. This is a wonderfully subtle process through which we build up our knowledge of the world by re-visiting our experiences in the light of new sense perceptions. Each new addition to our treasure trove of maps takes with it something of ourselves or, put another way, becomes a new part of ourselves. This gives our meaning to our experience.

Main Points Again

- Memories are complex and subtle mental maps, strongly coloured by the emotional experiences that accompany them.
- Memories personalize our life experience.

12. Mapping Qualities

If we want children to develop a real understanding of the world around them, they first have to discover and explore it and make a personal connection to it. This has its basis in the immediate world of things and phenomena around them. They also need to have a conceptual and literal vocabulary of what they know so they can think and talk about it.

Discovering the material qualities of their environment, their smells, sounds, textures, weight, consistency, and so on contributes to an ever-expanding catalogue of variable and multi-sensory experiences. This also includes qualities such as sticky, brittle, reflective, elastic, soft, dark, and so on – all qualities which can be applied not only to a range of materials in different states but can also in due course be used in a transferable, metaphorical sense. The world of material qualities also provides us with a vocabulary for imaginative, poetic, and psychological concepts.

The expressions, 'she was in a sticky situation', 'his argument was flaky', or 'there was a fragile peace', all depend for their effect on us being familiar with the original physical qualities. Such familiarity is established through the young child's exploratory play and questioning activity. The child continuously asks questions through her activity along the lines of, 'Can I walk on it?'; 'What happens if I try to bend it?'; 'Can I drink it?' When these questions are explored in context – that is, as they arise in the course of play or life generally – the lessons learned can be increasingly applied to new situations.

If we direct the child away from experiential learning to artificial learning situations, we may increase the vocabulary, but the experience that stands behind the word may remain tenuous. A book illustration of a bumblebee gives only a visual representation, usually out of context, sitting there on its own on a white page. The concept is not anchored in a multi-sensory context, such as a child would have in the garden. Such representations are only really useful if they serve to relate a story, or when the child can compensate for the lack of sensory context from her wealth of real experience. Books are best used to remind us and sometimes to clarify what we have already experienced or when we have enough experience, to imagine what the image might be like in reality. It is better to know your back yard well than to look at pictures of the Grand Canyon. If we have climbed on rocks, clambered up steep dusty banks, seen blood-red sunsets, then the photograph of the Grand Canyon will be far more evocative.

The transition from specific perceptions to general concepts is significant. Talking about things, giving them names, discussing their range of qualities (characterizing how a plant looks at different times of the year, how animals behave, what materials are used for, and so on) is the essential next step. Only when the child can visualize things when they are *not there*, and imagine things they have never seen, can one meaningfully move on to understanding things in a causal way. As we have stressed elsewhere, the mood we evoke in talking about such things is also important. Wonder is the basis of good science.

To provide abstract concepts before the child has experienced them directly, or can visualize them in their imagination, places a filter on the experience. To explain to a young child that the moon is a dead lump of rock held between the Earth and Sun by gravity will not fit easily with what she experiences when she peeps through the curtains at a rising harvest moon. If instead we can reinvoke our own childhood wonder at the moon and communicate *this* mood in whatever we actually say to our enquiring child, then we shall be confirming a reality for that child. The truth that young children seek is the truth of feelings, not the truth of concepts abstracted from the heart.

Main Points Again

- Memories that are imbued with feelings of love, respect, and wonder form a moral undertone to the individual's inner life in later years.
- Memories woven through with imagination provide the healthy basis for scientific knowledge.

13. Mapping Relationships

Another important phase of mapping involves becoming aware of human relationships. The young child will build up a memory of familiar people in a generalized way. The selection process is so open, in fact, that most young children will be comfortable with strangers unless they behave in unfamiliar or unpredictable ways, or unless the parents give off warning signals and treat the newcomer with caution. Children from a very early age are able to read very subtle signs of behaviour and often pick up on clues that indicate nervousness, uncertainty, or annoyance (though they don't always respond in appropriate or tactful ways.) The ability to 'read' the range of gestures and tones that other people make is not the same as understanding them. We could call this the first 'reading' of emotional language. The mapping of these signs is probably only at a pre-conceptual level that simply indicates that certain body language gestures indicate friendliness or uncertainty. The child cannot yet understand *why* the person is behaving like that.

Relationships, however, become important information to map. At first these are associative – that is, they associate certain people with situations, such as associating Grandpa with his garden shed, or the neighbour with his big dog. Gradually the child can fill in some of the linking detail such as: that is Sandra's sister, or Jack and Jill live up the hill. It is rare that children grasp that Grandma is Mummy's mummy much before about 6 years of age. In play, relationships are usually concerned with playmates rather than friendships in the true sense. All these relationships are mapped in a concrete and practical way. Only much later when the soul forces are more developed do children begin to expand these maps with qualitative judgements.

With regard to the formation of mental mapping and representational processes, we propose to designate the complex of inner activity responsible for these as 'the body of formative forces'. We also contend that this same 'body of formative forces' is primarily active within the first six or seven years in building up the patterns and rhythms within and between the major organ systems. Especially important is the focus, differentiation, and integration of the sensory processes. This body of forces is wholly integrated within the physical structures, being the formative activity within growth and development itself. The child's experience of herself, her feeling for life, and her whole sense of well-being is wholly bound up with the physicality of her nature in the early years. In turn this means that experiences which cannot be assimilated (because they are abstract) consume forces of vitality rather than build them up. In a sense they are indigestible, like feeding on stones rather than bread.

Gradually the formative forces that underlie the earlier form of sense-related memory and representation become loosened from their initial bonding with the senses and the organic processes related to cognitive activity. This usually occurs between the ages of 6 and 8 years of age. The child is then able at will to form mental images of things independent of their full context. In other words the child can begin to visualize things not literally present and sense perceptible. This includes beginning to anticipate consequences of what might or could happen. Ultimately this means that the child can think in abstract, even hypothetical terms. This third stage of representation, following the mapping of *activity* and the mapping of *pictures*, can be called the mapping of *symbols*. This means that the child can begin to understand that symbols can represent activities (such as the '+' sign) or things (written words) and even sounds (letters and musical notation). Once this capacity has begun to show itself, the formal teaching of literacy and numeracy can and should begin effectively.

What happens if the formative forces within the child's being are called upon to form and relate to abstract symbols and concepts before they have begun to liberate themselves from the child's organism? That is a very difficult question to answer and we know of no physiological evidence to support any specific conclusions, though we would love to see scientists even acknowledge the validity of the question. However, as we said at the outset, we feel justified in inferring from the evidence of developing children that certain signs point toward the following provisional conclusion.

We suggest that, if these formative forces are called upon to process abstract concepts and symbols, the child will have greater difficulty relating these to her direct experience and their natural context. The child may be able to recognize and use symbols, but the experience associated with them, which makes them real and easily assimilated, relatable and retainable in memory, is missing or weak. In other words, the child will create meagre maps with few connections to represent them. This does not make the task of applying them to writing, reading, counting, or to the understanding of complex ideas easier but rather the opposite. If they do not mean much, they will not interest the child; in fact they may '*un-interest*' her. Many learning difficulties we encounter reflect a strong element of fear arising from confusion and over-taxation of unprepared faculties. Fear of failure among children who are developmentally unready for the challenges presented to them is a major cause for distress.

We must not overlook the amount of energy a child needs to think and learn. The mentally overtaxed child will lose vitality, enthusiasm, become pale and listless, and may even get stomach cramps with the effort. We can compare the healthy tiredness of a child returning from a day at the beach with the restless tiredness at the end of a busy day going in the car, sitting in school with lots of other stressed children and teachers! These symptoms of lowered vitality may, in addition to the effects mentioned, include a kind of non-specific anxiety that may, if unresolved, develop into serious neuroses during adolescence. Our message here is simple. We see early intellectual learning as both a short- and long-term physical health issue. At the same time we see it affecting both inner motivation and the very practical ability to learn.

Main Points Again

- The young child has no inherent feeling for 'stranger' but is acutely sensitive to any disturbance in the 'well-being' of her environment.
- People are first 'mapped' in their typical contexts.
- Only from around 6 years of age can the child visualize reality quite independently of sense experience.
- The ability to map symbols emerges from the mapping of real pictures and activities. The healthy teaching of literacy and numeracy depends on this being established.
- Premature intellectual demands may lead to loss of interest, confusion, and fatigue.

14. Computers

The issue of the use of computers by young children is a complex and emotive one. In this book we do not particularly wish to get too preoccupied with the topic, but there are a few points that we wish to make in relation to the theme of cognitive development and learning.

The first point has already been made: children need lots of direct experience of the world involving as many senses as possible in order to provide a richly textured basis for understanding what things are. It is obvious that sitting in front of a screen is very limiting in this respect. In the age of cyberspace it also becomes especially relevant that our children distinguish between the artificial world and the real one. Given the trust that children bring with them, the ability to discriminate between 'actual' and 'virtual' has to be based on experience and not just on being told matter of factly that cyber-reality is virtual – which is, even for adults, a highly misleading concept. It is in some way like the television/video discussion: it's not so much the content but the means of engagement, which leads to inner and outer passivity, that is the problem.

The next point really concerns the attitude that working or playing with a computer brings with it. Saying that the capacity to click our way through the stages of discovery involves low levels of thinking would be a gross understatement. When NASA trains pilots to fly the Space Shuttle, they start by teaching them to sail dinghies, so that they can get the feel for wind, currents, steering, tacking, and so on, as well as being able to navigate. They progress through larger sailing vessels to small aircraft and so on, up to the Shuttle itself. By the time they get to sitting in the Shuttle cockpit, there is no more wind to feel, only massive banks of dials and buttons to press. But knowing what the principles involved are, knowing how to navigate, means being able to interpret the options that the computers provide to the pilot, and thus makes them far better equipped to know what is *really* happening and what the consequences of problems might be. One can wonder what computer games involving car chases and painless crashes do for the driving skills of the younger generation and accident statistics.

A child does not need to know how computers work, or vacuum cleaners for that matter, to use them (though at an older age this is important too, for the same reason that NASA teaches its pilots about aerodynamics and propulsion). But she does need to know what the information really means. The mental effort involved in solving relevant problems creatively is up-building rather than tiring and strengthens cognitive processes. Children are not short of energy when they need it and are motivated to use it. The click culture leads to lazy thinking. The starting is often the actual problem. Children already have short attention spans and are often weak willed when it comes to their comfort. The educational psychologist Jane Healy described the situation as follows:

'Encouraging children to "learn" by flitting about in a colourful multi-media world is a recipe for a disorganised and undisciplined mind. Today's students are increasingly difficult to teach. Their learning habits have been shaped by fast-paced media that reduce attention, listening and problem-solving skills as they habituate the brain to rapid fire visual input.'[7]

Computers are windows that open not outward but inward, into the mental world of their creators. Getting into this world is simply a matter of learning how to operate the keys. If there is a way through this world to the real world outside, however, it is very much on the programmer's terms. We question whether young children are going to be able to meet these terms without enormous cost. Some may go in and come back out the way they came, which may be fine; others may go in and get lost and not come out the right way at all. Perhaps this sounds like scare-mongering, but the fact that computer programs now exist for 6-9 month-old babies must surely alert us to the possibility that something *could be* going badly wrong. We don't suppose that the Microsoft Corporation will be donating too much to this kind of research.

The argument that watching television or videos, or using compact discs or the internet, offers children the opportunity to immerse themselves in the world of orality (which we discuss in detail in Chapter 16, 'Tell Me a Story') is threadbare. Don't they get plenty of narrative and hear the human voice in recorded form? The reality is that no one using electronic media is really involved in conversation, for the basic principle of dialogue is mutuality, which includes the possibility of asking questions, interrupting, arguing, repeating, and so on – all typical features or real communication. Above all there is no inner commitment to a response. In true dialogue the speaker challenges the listener in principle to respond, or at least to engage. It requires an effort of will either to get involved or to turn away. Either way, the response is willed because of the physical presence of the other.

In electronic exchanges – and of course the software manufacturers are very aware of this and market so-called interactive programs – the will is not engaged, and there is no emotional commitment because there are no consequences. We all know the feeling when someone won't say to our faces what they really think but go behind our backs and tell others. We naturally feel offended by the lack of openness because we are denied the opportunity of perceiving for ourselves what the other really thinks or feels. This experience only highlights the qualitative difference between speaking to a real and unpredictable person and a software program.

We all know that sitting in front of a screen deprives children of time for valuable creative play, for being in nature, for reading, talking to people, being artistic, working, or – heaven forbid – just sitting quietly. We don't mean to be flippant in suggesting that young children don't really have time for sitting at computers. They will spend much of their adult lives, as indeed we do, doing just that, despite a later start!

In the next chapter we explore the vital role in the child's learning experience of healthy play.

Children ' should have a book at bedtime, not TV'. The danger which television poses to children was highlighted again yesterday by a major study showing how it can cause serious sleep disorders. Youngsters are less likely to sleep soundly if they watch TV just before going to bed, according to research carried out in the U.S. Doctors from the American Academy of Paediatrics warned that allowing a child to have a television set in his or her bedroom was 'a slippery slope'. The academy, which has 55,000 members, caused a storm last month when it said children under two should not watch television at all because it can harm their development.

Ian Cobain, *Daily Mail*, Thursday 9th September 1999

It is a bizarre coincidence, and a foreboding one, that just as Tony Blair is trumpeting his plan to wire up every British schoolchild to a computer, evidence is accumulating in the United States that high tech classrooms cause more harm than good... There is a move away from the education traditions that encouraged students to rely on their brains and five senses, and developed their abilities to communicate insightfully with people. And it is a move towards reliance on a machine, which too often dumbs down children's thinking rather than expanding it.

Todd Oppenheimer, Associate Editor of Newsweek,
The Guardian, 8th October 1997

15. Play with a Purpose

The phrase 'child's play' is normally used to suggest that something is easy. Anyone observing a child playing however, will concede that if an adult were to work with the same concentration, devotion, and enthusiasm, he or she would be in line for promotion.

It would not be inappropriate to say that in playing, the child is also working for her own promotion. In this sense play should be taken seriously by adults as well as children. The more interest we take in our children's play, the more we shall understand their needs and purposes. The games children play, as with the pictures they draw, are illuminations of an inner developmental intention at work.

What is the first experience we could call 'child's play'? Consider the way an infant 'roots' for the breast at the touch of her cheek. This is obviously not a deliberate act, nor one that the baby can deliberately refuse. The rules of the rooting game, if we want to call it that, are very clear: be touched and you must chase the toucher. Later in life the same game will be played, but then we shall call it 'tig'.

At the basis of both 'rooting' and 'tig' lies the sense of touch. Through touch we both meet the world and begin to learn our difference from the world. We sometimes speak of a 'playful touch' in contrast to a 'heavy touch'. A child's first touching is playful, not merely because a child is more thin-skinned and sensitive than an adult but because her touching involves a particularly active and continuous interchange between her inner and outer experience. Without this 'on/off' reciprocation she would lose her sense of having an experience at all. A dog following a scent has to 'cast' to either side of it because an unmitigated sense impression becomes dulled and ultimately disappears from awareness altogether.

All play has at its heart a process of rhythmic interchange. The play of light and shadow, the 'playing' of a fish, the play shared between actors and audience, the playing of music: all these are experiences in which different elements of the 'total' experience are continually changing places. Play (so closely related in early childhood to touching) could be described as a rhythmic process of communion – as important to the child as religion may be to an adult.

The way we allow and encourage children to play is of spiritual concern. The health of the body; the life processes; mental, emotional, social, and moral competence; and conscience and the innermost sense of self – all are developed through play. Sometimes the child herself will need to be the main player; sometimes she will need to play with other children; sometimes she will need to play with us. Getting this right is as important as any other educational measure we might devise.

During the first two years of play the child begins to understand the objects and activities of her world. This is a constant voyage of discovery – a journey with only the barest of maps provided by the relatively few real instincts with which human beings are born. Everything at this stage is of equal interest and significance. The baby wants to touch and taste it all because she expects it all to be good.

Amongst the baby's earliest playthings are her own hands and feet. The first encounter between right and left hand is an accident. The more often the accident happens the more aware of it and interested the baby becomes. And now the one hand starts to play with the other, as it would appear. In reality the baby is playing with both her hands as if they were foreign objects. Yet through the process of touching and losing touch the child is slowly learning to 'make touch' deliberately, and in this way to identify and locate the 'furniture' of her world.

If the baby's hands and feet become less foreign the more she plays with them, it is also the case that separate objects become experienced as 'more like baby' the more she plays with them. Her cot and blankets, mobile and rattle become, through play, like further sets of arms and legs. If these are taken away from her she experiences, albeit only momentarily, a kind of identity crisis.

Child development books often describe that infants at this early stage have no sense of 'object permanence'. This means that, if a plaything is taken out of a baby's reach and perception, the baby will almost immediately carry on with something else as if the object had never even been there in the first place. This, however, should not be an excuse for insensitively changing the baby's world around it, because 'object permanence' is actually the name of the infant's game. The re-appearance of familiar objects and sights are an important preparation for forgetting and remembering.

Once again, it is a question of balance. One of the youngster's favourite games is '*peep-bo*'. This is a game where a key feature of reality – the human face – is deliberately removed out of the baby's world, and then suddenly popped back into it. The sheer delight with which the baby greets this sudden reappearance is the equivalent on a now more conscious level of the delight with which she has always greeted her milk. The removal of the face, we might say, causes a form of soul hunger, and the returning face satisfies the soul and strengthens its interest in life. The art of playing this game successfully is the art of timing. One child will differ from another, and will itself change along the way, in just how long it can sustain its active anticipation before the 'Bo!' fulfils it again, rather than simply drifting off to other things.

Another development of *peep-bo*, often less popular with parents, is the game of dropping toys off the high chair and, with increasing deliberateness, expecting them to be put back up again. Like *peep-bo* this is a game which confirms the child's reality. It is also a game through which the child learns to play a more active role in the arrangement of reality, and most importantly of all, in integrating herself with other human beings. Frustrating and time-consuming as it may be, these interactive games are crucial to the child's well-being and advancement, and should never be misinterpreted as mere wilfulness. Neither should we misinterpret the youngster's inclination to build things and then to delight in knocking them down, only to want to build them up again. This is a game we could call 'digestion', because it is a parallel version of the metabolic activity through which 'world' becomes 'child'.

The culmination of this first whole period of play normally comes somewhere in the second year, when the child is really ready to distinguish and play with a human doll. Earlier we said that everything which the child first learns to identify through its senses and movements is experienced as a part of its own being. The most readily accessible feature of reality in this sense is the mother, followed by the other members of the family, other human beings, and then animals and the other living things of nature.

The doll is not animate but the child can make it animate, as she (and here we had better specifically emphasize 'he' as well) can with anything else. What distinguishes the doll from other kinds of plaything is that it presents itself in human form, which the child can take hold of (literally) and make her own. Somewhere toward her third year the child will be ready to focus on the possibilities that go along with this. But in order for these possibilities to be fully available to her – or him! – the doll itself should be as soft, rounded, and dreamy as the child herself. Because this is who the doll is.

Like everyone and everything else, the doll is experienced by the infant as an extension of her being; but the doll has the special possibility of representing this being in its true and childlike earthly representation. This is not a being who is yet fully formed or who has yet hardened its body. For this reason a plastic doll with sophisticated features is not what the child is looking for. What the child wants is something which can reflect her own condition and her own continuing possibilities of development. She will find this in a doll made of soft and natural material which can snuggle in her arms as she herself snuggles in her mother's arms. The doll need have no more than the archetypal intimation, the simplest hint, of a face, which can then be pictured in whatever expression the child's mood is asking for. Better one such doll than a catalogue display of perhaps expensive but ultimately unsatisfying offerings such as our consumer culture is only too happy to provide. This is not to deny that children need more than dolls to play with. The point being made is that a child should have a family of toys that she can relate to as part of her family and part of herself.

With her emergent self-image (compare her cross drawn in the circle) the child is now ready to play seriously at being grown-up. This can of course be taxing for the real grown-ups, as when Daddy is up the ladder or ironing and someone else wants to do it too... As with the earlier child's play, however, it is important that adults are willing to join in. The child is declaring her readiness not simply to be part of the family but also to help keep house because this is what families do. Play is now about work – active, sociable, homely work.

Of course human beings do far less of this kind of manual maintenance work than in earlier times, which is a great pity for our children. Even if we belong to a world where machines do a great deal of the work for us, we need to go through what it means to work in a hands-on way if we are to experience our own human possibilities to the full, and a wholesome relation to the earth on which we live. The young child is drawn to imitate activity. If she cannot find much human activity to reproduce she will attempt to reproduce other activities – like the washing machine, the vacuum cleaner, the television. And this has enormous potential to disturb and disrupt her development.

Observing and imitating human work and care for the domestic environment gives the child a significant moral example for life. The activities of washing, cleaning, gardening etc. are humanized, economic, efficient, and kinaesthetic – beautiful in their movements. If pleasure is taken in the task it becomes meaningful, a real deed of caring, rather than a necessary chore. It is an act of conscious service, which requires both skill and perseverance. Of course there is no ethic in drudge, but there is an ethic in conscious ecological care for the environment.

A period of some relief normally begins to dawn for the parents and carers as the child approaches her fourth year. A new faculty is beginning to emerge out of the imitative communion with the world. We could call this faculty fantasy. It is the child's ability to project her increasingly conscious inner life on to the world around her. This is a magical power: she can turn the floor into an ocean, the chair into a boat; or suddenly it is a throne for a princess, and now a pony... Again, the child is taking hold of the world and then letting it go; experiencing its (and her own) possibilities but not liking to get stuck with them for too long.

A distinguishing feature of this fantasy play is that it requires props. The things of the world are still a necessary part of the magic spell. And some things are innately more magical than others. Pebbles are more magical than Lego blocks because they are easier to change into other things – say bread buns, gold coins, houses, hills. At this stage we serve the child well by offering a ready supply of such props – including, from time to time, ourselves.

Through this fantasy stage the child begins to explore new possibilities of playing with other children. To begin with, the youngster may have been happy to play simply in the company of other children, alongside but not necessarily much involved with them. The enchantment of play seems to have a special attraction, but the challenge of having two or more magicians working on the same spell initially proves to be too much. Nevertheless, it is precisely this challenge that the soul of the child is seeking, and that she needs to resolve.

Children find each other in play. A group of four or five year olds can achieve an astonishing harmony and creativity in their make-believe. They can equally impressively fall out over it. But this is not a time for lasting grudges. The children are not yet meeting each other as individuals but rather as playmates. If the game of the moment needs someone to play a particular role in it, the need to fill the role is more important than who fills the role. This is a social education that will never again be so rich in possibilities. How ready are we in adult life to offer other people, whom we perhaps don't personally like very much, important tasks which they will need encouragement and help to fulfil? The fact that we are ready to do so at all is a gift of our childhood. In return we should encourage and assist (but not impose) the development of sociability through play.

The games children play at this age are often fantasies based on imitation, although frequently they are inspired by stories and other imaginations that have come to them. This openness to inspiration needs to be nourished in a healthy way. The simpler folk tales and fairy tales offer by far the best kind of imaginative fertilization. Biographical accounts of what the grown-ups did as children are also good. Nature nurtures the child's imagination too, of course.

Another developing feature of the children now is their love for song, dance, rhythmic gestures, and movements of all kinds. They will endlessly and tirelessly chant the same things over and over again. They will play the same games over and over again. They will want the same stories over and over again – exactly as they heard them before. And we must do our best to grant them this wish. It is a wish that comes straight from the heart, which at this time of life is still learning to establish its own rhythms. The rhythm of the heart is the basis for physical and emotional health; it is also the basis for counting, making music, and – crucially – remembering. The activities and games that express the heart are also games that develop the heart, together with the whole of our rhythmic system and the capacities that belong with it.

As the child approaches the end of the garden path of childhood the purpose in her play changes. Hitherto her playing has been very much a thing of the moment – a spontaneous interaction with whatever and whoever happens to be there to play with. Now, around the sixth year, the activity of play begins to be more deliberate and consequent. Games are intended and planned; they are remembered from one day to the next; the children are more specific and choosy in the way they are played and in the choice of who plays them.

The typical six year old is more interested in creating a reality through play, whereas a five year old is happier to adapt and adapt to the reality that is there. The six year old's play has become more inward. Fewer props are needed to make it work, and the props that are used must be good enough not to destroy the illusion that the inner world is as real as the outer world. Images become imagination and story begins.

No healthy six year old *really* believes that the world of her make-believe is the same as the objective world she shares with the grown-ups; but she does, and must, believe that her inner world is as real as her own inner being. Her ultimate aim is to unite this inner world with the outer world so that what she really wants can be really true. She wants to live in the world of possibilities as well as the world of rationality. The rich creativity of this period can provide the driving force for a whole life!

This underlying impulse to transform the world to suit the child's inner needs is a dynamic and creative power. Children who are allowed to play freely will demonstrate a genius for lateral thinking and problem solving of which we adults should be envious. All too often, unfortunately, well-intentioned adults are too quick to intervene with their own less-inspired contributions, and on both sides important possibilities remain unrealized.

Having said this, the child can become increasingly frustrated that she can't achieve her desired objectives in the way that adults seem able to do. A related threshold period of idealism and frustration will come to her again with puberty. During both these periods of transition it is especially important that the child's self-esteem and enthusiasm are kept intact.

With this in mind the question of a five or six year old's readiness for formal education needs to be considered very carefully.

Ready to Help? – Five and Six Year Olds

It is sometimes the case that children appear ready both in their physical and cognitive development to start explicit learning at school. Before sending them off to school, please consider the following.

Learning to read, write, and do arithmetic involves the children in directing their will into their thinking. They have to do this in order to be able to focus on the meaning of the symbols they have to use, otherwise their dream-like minds would simply proceed associatively, as in free play. The thinking necessary for literacy is a great focuser.

What happens if we don't engage their wills in thinking? If

instead we channel it into shaping and forming their feeling life, we will be doing them a service. It is our feeling life that provides us with the basis for forming relationships, for empathizing with and caring for others, both of which require will power, but not in the head. We can strengthen children's feeling life by encouraging them in this last phase of early childhood to help those younger than themselves, care for their environment, and generally be helpful. In kindergarten in particular, these five and six year olds can willingly be a great help, taking on all kinds of tasks for the community and deriving real pleasure from them.

Another aspect of the feeling life is forming the basis for aesthetic appreciation. By caring for the appearance of things, by helping to arrange the seasonal table, setting the meal table, folding napkins, making flower displays, exploring colour, and generally caring for the environment in small but 'felt' ways, these children establish inner habits which will serve them (and others) well during the rest of their lives.

If sensitivity toward other people and the environment is not well developed early on, the child may struggle to find equilibrium later. If the will forces flow directly into thinking, unmediated by the life of feeling and aesthetic judgement, this can manifest as selfishness, self-centredness, and nervousness later in life. Furthermore, the ability to form subtle judgements, rather than jumping to quick, rational conclusions, may be weakened.

The inability of many adolescents, and adults for that matter, to be able to empathize with others or form meaningful relationships may relate to the fact that their feeling life remained undeveloped because it was overtaken by premature intellectuality. This is more the case with boys, who are often not encouraged to care for others or their environment as girls are. Boys are allowed to 'be boys' and are often not expected to develop any aesthetic sense in childhood. All children need caring role models, especially during this age of imitation and habit building – but boys need it more.

The moral consequences of delaying formal learning at school until the conclusion of the first seven-year period was clearly a priority in Rudolf Steiner's thinking, and has remained so within the Steiner Waldorf schools movement ever since. The findings of the High/Scope Project referred to earlier (see Chapter 2) endorse *this* factor more strongly even than the questionable academic advantage of any accelerated learning approach.

Main Points Again

- 'Child's play' is a serious business.
- Playing has a spiritual developmental purpose.
- 'Child's play' begins with touch.
- Playful touching involves a rhythmic reciprocal interchange between 'self' and 'other'.
- Play may reveal a religious significance within the child's consciousness.
- Creating appropriate opportunities for play at the right times is an educational measure of crucial importance.
- Play begins as a confident journey of discovering the outer world.
- The child first discovers its own body as part of the outer world.
- As the child makes contact with the world through play she also begins to identify the world as part of herself.
- Continuity within the child's environment helps develop continuity of self.
- Games like 'peep-bo' help develop an inner capacity for 'object-permanence'.
- More self-directed losing and recovering, or breaking and remaking games, are part of the child's discovery of self-control and control of the world.
- Readiness to play with a doll marks a new step toward independence.
- Children reveal a natural hierarchy of interest stretching between human beings and lifeless immobile objects.

- The child's potential is to animate the doll with her (or his) own being.
- The doll itself should initially reflect a childlike quality.
- The child increasingly imitates the activities going on around her.
- The child is best served when she has wholesome human activities to imitate.
- Fantasy begins to develop out of simple imitation.
- Initially fantasy games spring from real-life situations and require physical props to support them.
- Fantasy becomes a medium for social play.
- Children need, meet, develop, and respect each other as playmates.
- Children's fantasy is enriched by hearing appropriate stories.
- A growing musicality inspires delight in rhythmic singing and action games.
- Toward the sixth year a new faculty of inner purpose begins to direct the child's play.
- Fantasy develops into imagination, where inner images are independently created and actively projected on to the world.
- Make-believe is not an escape from reality but an attempt to change it for the better.
- Creative play develops creative problem-solving.
- Frustrations also develop toward the seventh year in a kind of 'first puberty'.
- Encouraging helpfulness can strengthen the bond between willing and feeling, establishing the basis for both social and aesthetic development.
- This has a special relevance for boys.

Practical Considerations

The way our children play says as much about adults as children. Adults make and market children's toys. They are also the ones who buy the toys, rarely uninfluenced by the sales hype that their children have swallowed.

Hard-pressed parents can't help welcoming opportunities for a break from hassle, and getting their children to play with anything and anyone but themselves can be too attractive to want to question very closely. And the children do seem to be enjoying themselves... just as they seem to enjoy junk food. But healthy food and healthy play is something more. Luckily, once it's established it's lovely to observe and be part of. What threatens it more than anything is inertia – and that's something we can change.

Life is too hard, according to *Listening to Four Year Olds*, a study published by the National Early Years Network. About 130 children in this survey told the researcher, Dr Jacqui Cousins, that they were constantly being told to hurry up, that they were swotting for their Key Stage One tests, that they were bedevilled by the concept of 'end-product activities' and 'learning outcomes', that as nursery school ended, the ballet, music and art classes began. These are children born to parents whose idea of doing the best for them is to cram them into the right nursery school for the right primary school for the right secondary or public school, children who left the womb to be strapped to the hamster wheel of activity. ...Because parents are so hard-pressed themselves, so pressured to do and achieve, they have forgotten that play can be the best of all modes of being. Any artist and many scientists could tell you that real creativity comes out of play. By play I mean an activity undertaken for its own sake and fascination, having no fixed end but being an enthralling journey, and often resulting in some new discovery or the development of a new skill.

Lesley Garner, 'What Pushy Parents Need – a Few Mud Pies', *Evening Standard*, Monday 14th June 1999

16. Tell Me a Story: The Meaning of the Spoken Word

Understanding without Words

Mara's mother is German, her father English. They live in England and speak English at home. In the summer, when Mara was just two and a bit, the family went to stay with the German grandparents, neither of whom speak English. The parents were a little concerned about how Mara would manage, as she was beginning to form simple sentences in English. Would she understand? Would she get confused? Might she even be set back in her language development? The following situation unfolded.

After a couple of days, during which either mother or father were around to interpret, Grandmother suggested that while the parents went into town shopping, Mara could stay with her and help in the garden. After a moment of hesitation, the parents willingly agreed, and departed, leaving Mara in the capable hands of Oma. On their return Grandmother explained that everything had worked out fine. In fact, she had been somewhat astonished that dealing with Mara was linguistically no more difficult than dealing with her German grandchildren. Apparently Mara had not only accompanied Oma picking beans, grasped which ones to pick and which ones to leave, but had even followed instructions (now translated into English) such as: 'Go and put those into the basket'; 'No, we don't need to pull up the carrots'; and 'Go into the kitchen and put the cup on the table'.

In the case of the first two instructions, some gesture played a part, such as pointing to the basket, which already contained beans, or a shake of the head and hand in the direction of the beans. The kitchen table was not, however, visible and the instruction about the cup could not be pantomimed, according to Oma, because her hands were full at the time.

The experience of communicating without spoken language is quite familiar from travel to foreign countries. We can probably recall doing things such as purchasing fruit in a market in Turkey without a word of Turkish. Many things are possible without a common language and it is worth reflecting on what they involve.

Gesture and body language are remarkably effective at communicating intentions. A good mime artist can entertain us for an hour and tell a long and complex story. In ordinary conversation between adults, up to 80 per cent of what is understood by the partners in dialogue is non-semantic, that is to say is not communicated by the actual words spoken but by non-verbal means, which includes tone and intonation of voice, along with gesture and body language. This indicates that we have the capacity to perceive, even in a sequence of meaningful movements, the thought contained within them.

Pointing

Pointing is a symbolic gesture that is an important precursor of language. The following experiment makes this clear.

A child is placed in a high chair in front of a table. There's a video behind a window to record the event, wired up with various sensors. Mother puts a favourite teddy bear or drinking cup or biscuit on a table just out of reach. A group of neuro-scientists, developmental psychologists, and social anthropologists huddle round the monitor, but the child is blissfully unaware of them. The child has far more important matters to deal with, namely getting at the object of her desire. At first, straining forward in the straps, little hands reach out to grasp the object, putting the whole wiring arrangement at some risk. This is followed by imploring gestures of the hands, followed shortly by an upward and backward arching of the back, stretching of the legs, opening of the mouth, and the letting forth of a penetrating squeal of pain, turning into a yell, with the whole chair in danger of overturning.

At a certain point the child changes her tactic. She begins to stretch out, not her whole grasping hand, but starts to point to the object with her index finger, whilst looking expectantly from the object to the mother and back again. At the same time the whole activity is accompanied by the mouthing of sounds. Boris Cyrulink, the neurologist who describes this experiment, calls this the moment

> 'that the child attempts, invariably failing at first, to articulate a word. I have ventured to coin a word to designate this failed word: I call it a "proto-word"; we perceive it as an acoustic emission sounding like "bah-bah". It leads us to the beginnings of symbolism and the origin of the ability to evoke absent objects.'[8]

This marvellous little moment is of huge significance, probably repeated many times unnoticed by busy parents. The gesture is not merely directing attention, it represents the object in the sense of the word 'that' in the sentence 'I want that'. Furthermore, the child is entering into a complex negotiation with the mother. The child wants the mother to do something on *her* behalf. On top of which, the movement toward the object, which of necessity is restrained by straps, is converted into the forming of sounds, into proto-words which, if 'translated', would say, 'I want that biscuit now very much, yes that one right there on the table over there, the one with the sticky bits of chocolate in it which I like, don't I?' Of course, if the child actually had the right words, she would probably only simply say, 'Biscuit! Mummy!' The rest would be implicit.

What this experiment and the story about Mara show us is that language operates at many levels and that the learning of it reveals something of these levels. The story of Mara and her grandmother shows us that children understand the intentions of adults even if they don't literally grasp the meaning of the words. The conditions have to be right. The child must feel comfortable with the adult, must already be familiar with the situation to some extent, the adult must focus on communicating with the child and keep things relatively transparent but not necessarily simple. This works best if the activity involved is concrete and of shared meaning. Mara imitates not only how her grandmother acts, the rapid but selective probing of size and firmness, picking the beans and dropping them carefully into the basket; she also becomes so absorbed in the activity that she also imitates the mood of matter-of-fact concentration, the satisfaction of the experienced gardener, as well as repeating the words (in German as it happens) for picking beans, which the grandmother stresses in unobtrusive 'motherese'.

Motherese

'Motherese' is the term given by developmental linguists to the way of speaking mothers (and others) generally use when speaking to young children. As it happens, motherese is also used between lovers and when people speak to animals. This is not, as one might think, baby talk, though very young babies do get quite a lot of this, without seriously hindering their subsequent ability to speak correctly. In fact, motherese consists mostly of highly intelligible sentences with a bona fide grammatical structure, the rest being well formed isolated phrases. The sentences are shorter and clearer than normal speech, avoiding complex grammatical structures, but do not over-simplify.

Research[9] has shown that what is considered to be the basic and simplest forms of sentence structure in English, namely sentences that have the subject-verb-object form, do not predominate in motherese. In conversation between adults this form accounts for up to 87 per cent of sentences. Motherese is far more varied; only 30 per cent have the subject-verb-object form, 44 per cent are questions, and 18 per cent are imperatives. Motherese is shorter and clearer but not simpler. Furthermore, parents do not match the complexity of sentences to the developmental stage of the child (even developmental linguists apparently don't do this either), nor is there any obvious correlation between the complexity of parental language and the child's own progress in mastering the language.

This casts doubt on the assertion that learning language structure, or indeed any subsequent foreign languages, depends upon what might be considered logical rules of progressing from simple to complex, introducing one new construction at a time and starting with subject-verb-object sentences. Motherese does none of these things, which suggests that children do not learn the structure of their mother tongue by systematic imitation or that they are taught systematically by their well-trained parents. There is a considerable difference between parental input and the child's utterances. The fact is that children do not learn their first language through the systematic learning of rules as an anthropologist from Mars might suppose. However, it *is* clear that there are certain key elements of language that children can only learn from those around them.

The apocryphal story of the Egyptian Pharaoh who, wishing to discover the origin of human language, ordered two children to be brought up by a goat herd far from human society and with strict instructions not to speak to them, highlights this in a curious way. After growing up in this isolated place with only the goats for company, the scholars sent to investigate returned to report that the children's first words could be transcribed as '*bek-bek*'. Further research showed that this was close to the Syrian word for bread and so Syrian was declared to be the original human language. One suspects that the Pharaoh had some kind of Syrian heritage.

Children do imitate what they hear, and if that is only goats then the story is hardly surprising. What do children imitate then? They have the capacity to imitate all the sounds they hear around them but are nevertheless predisposed to respond most directly to human speech, and thereafter to other animate sounds. The specific speech sounds, as well as the melody, pitch, and intonation of the mother tongue make distinct impressions. We also know[10] that in listening to speech we imitate the movements made by the vocal tract of the speaker, which includes the muscles of the larynx, the tongue, and mouth, in micro-movements in our own speech apparatus. In fact, slowed-down film of people listening to speech reveals that these micro-movements in the form of ripples pass right through the face, throat, and trunk of the listener, mirroring those of the speaker. In the very young child these movements are even more pronounced and can even be observed as gentle murmurings and lip movements. A sudden cry or shout can make a child's muscle system jerk in a dramatic way.

As well as imitating the distinctive sounds and intonations of a regional accent, for example, the child also obviously copies the names for things and activities. Learning the grammatical structure of the native language is, however, another matter. Huge quantities of paper have been printed with research and theories to explain how children acquire this most essential aspect of language, and it would be fair to say that the matter has not been conclusively explained.

Language Development and the Nature of the Human Being

There are three basic theories that account for how language structure is acquired, and they swing in and out of fashion. They are important to our theme because each one implicitly says something about the nature of the human being and human development which has a wider significance than language acquisition. The first hypothesizes some kind of innate language acquisition system (genetically predetermined or otherwise), which assumes a universal structure common to all human languages and which enables each individual child to identify and learn the structure of his or her mother tongue. The main arguments for this (Chomskian or Nativist) theory include the view that the time needed by most children is too short, the structure too complex to be learned as a skill, the example provided even by motherese too inexact and unsystematic for this miracle to occur unless we are born with it more or less intact. This view of the human being places the emphasis on innate factors; the essentials are already there and need unpacking. Though Chomsky refuses to this day to be pinned down as to whether 'innate' here means genetic, the trend these days is to see what Steven Pinker termed a 'language instinct' at work.[11]

The main alternative, not much in vogue these days, is that we are born with a blank mind, the famous *tabula rasa*, and we systematically learn the language we hear through imitation and teaching. This so-called *Empiricist* view of the human being reached its most complete expression in the days of Behaviourism, when the human being was seen as a deficient creature, lacking the kind of instincts we find in animals and therefore not only susceptible to, but needing instruction. Children should therefore be moulded into shape and given experiences they need to develop the faculties they should have. This view stresses the acquisition of habits and a systematic or logical increment of tasks. This kind of approach is that of computer programming since the computer is the ultimate *tabula rasa*. The computing models of the brain are basically instructionist, as is software for educational use – click on *this* icon and *that* happens. It has to be said that if the Government has any educational theory underpinning its policies these would have to be described as instructionist in tenor. Their utilitarian approach of moving from simple to less simple, and doing what (apparently) works first, is a pattern found throughout the National Curriculum.

The third model of language acquisition which tells us about the nature of the developing human being is the *Interactionist* view, which in multiple versions envisages a bit of both *Nativist* and *Instructionist* approaches. On this kind of view, there is some form of innate predisposition, but without imitation and structured learning, little would come of it. The most fruitful versions of this approach see the process of language acquisition as an active interaction between child and adult, what is known as the interactionist approach. There is a noble tradition of Interactionism leading from the Russian Lev Vygotsky, through the American Jerome Bruner to the Englishman Gordon Wells[12], which offers a far more subtle picture of developmental processes which stress both the importance of maturational timetables and interactive learning. This approach, for example, stresses the strategies that children develop for themselves to bootstrap their own development, and in particular emphasizes the reciprocity in learning between children and adults and children and other children.

Any approach, such as our own, which attempts to include a spiritual element in human development must align itself with (and in some respects extend) the interactionist view of human life. What language acquisition and development reveal, together with many other aspects of development we refer to in this book, is the *self-activity* of the child. This activity, which engages in a process of taking hold of, mastering, and ultimately individualizing the native language, seems to us to be ultimately inexplicable in purely materialistic terms – including a materialistic form of interactionism. In our view it is an activity of the human spirit. Spirit is in this sense what happens between the words and between people when they communicate with each other; it lies in the intention within the meaning we seek to communicate. It is also what makes each voice unique.

At the same time we want to propose a further, perhaps more radical dimension to the spirituality of language – namely, that it represents an *objective* spiritual entity with its own inherent activity. This living spirit of language bears within it the profound and articulate wisdom of reality plus the formative power to shape and transform the thinking of those who 'use' it. Both the sounds of the vowels and consonants that make up spoken language and the syntactical structures that underlie all languages are archetypal in character. The use of language in this sense unites the spiritual activity of individuals with each other and with the spiritual activity of the world.

It is not possible within this book to look in detail at language acquisition, and the interested reader is advised to turn to some of the literature recommended in the bibliography. There are, however, some aspects that are of practical interest to us. In order to do this it is first necessary to characterize some of the qualities that human language possesses which are rarely taken into account.

Dialogue

Language for the child is primarily a means of communication and self-expression. Right from birth the child seeks communicative contact with those around her but essentially the mother. One could also argue that the child has been communicating its advent and its pre-natal existence to the parents for some time before birth. It is possible for mothers to have a sense of the impending coming of the child at the earliest stages of pregnancy and *even earlier*. We should not dismiss such intimations as sentimental, illusory, wishful thinking, or hindsight. In a very real sense the child has chosen to come to us as parents and this mystery is a form of dialogue. Both parents and child will have to continue this dialogue for many years to come. The questions, 'Why you?' 'Why me?' do not, as a rule, have obvious answers: long-term dialogue will be needed in all kinds of subtle ways if we are even to approach answers.

Of course there is also a wonderful and often painful dialogue between the unborn child and her mother. The child makes demands and has needs, and the mother responds, which we can call 'dialogue' because two sentient beings are relating and the outcome is not predictable. Much of this kind of dialogue remains unconscious even for the mother, but so do many other kinds of communication between people in life.

The post-natal communication channels announce themselves early on. The time immediately following the birth can often include moments in which the main players take a long deep look at each other before more pressing matters of sleep, comfort, and nourishment take over. Once the child is awake, she learns to focus very quickly and seeks eye contact. She responds quickly to familiar voices with pleasure, and demands attention in unmistakable terms. The urge we have to sing to our infants, to speak to them, even when rationally we may 'know' that they cannot possibly understand, are still powerful even in our rational times, thank goodness. One need only reflect on the terrible consequences of not doing so to appreciate why this is so vital. Many of us will remember the reports of those orphans in the Rumanian orphanages during the Ceaucescu era who, deprived of affection, attention, and conversation, were developmentally inhibited in profound ways, including physically, despite having in many cases been well-nourished and sheltered. It was not food which these tragic children needed but *dialogue*. The human being needs to be spoken to, addressed, conversed with as a primary developmental need.

In balance with peace and quiet, babies also need to be part of the community, to be around when others laugh and play and sing, or simply chat. At a few months, babies generally like nothing better than to be safely on someone's arm in the midst of social intercourse. We can well recall seeing happy babies lying on a rug on the kitchen floor, surrounded by dogs, cats, children, and adults coming and going. Yes, it probably was unhygienic, but those babies are now strapping young men and women. The point is that children need to be part of a real communicating community.

The best advice one can give parents of young children with regard to their language development is to speak to them and with them as often as opportunity arises. Don't train them, don't speak baby-talk. It won't do any harm but it won't make them feel better or learn faster. Provide them with opportunity to hear the human voice in all its rich diversity, and that includes the various languages that can be heard in the family. Don't offer them recorded human voices as a substitute. There are many reasons for this, but the main one is that the child needs to make many complex observations about vocal language production, let alone structure. We evolved highly sensitive organs to perceive these. No forms of recorded speech can transmit the full range of tones, frequencies, breathing patterns, facial movements, and vitality of live human speech or real interchange – someone who will respond. They have little time in which optimally to acquire all the basics. We complicate their task by flooding them with auditory or visual impressions they don't yet have the equipment to deal with. Moreover, spoken language contains vital elements that need to be perceived apart from the sounds and intonations.

Narrative as Meaning Making

Chatter is an early form of what later emerges as narrative, stories in which the child describes what she is doing, what happens, what she sees and hears. This is later complemented by retrospective stories which put everything into the past tense and imaginative excursions into what the child will do, would like to do, hopes will happen, and so on. Stories link the past, present, and future into an integrated whole.

This narrative is also a form of dialogue. Initially the narrative is actually self-directed, seeking only periodic confirmation from the participating adult: 'Yes, you did see that big dog at the street corner. It was barking, wasn't it? But it was all right because its Daddy came and took it home.' These affirmations not only reassure the child, they also help clarify the situation by leading the child to a happy conclusion as well as providing good linguistic models which the child will notice; and in repeating the sentence themselves the child corrects or varies the sentence structure.

This kind of narrative dialogue is invaluable for the child in many ways, and the complexity of the narrative structures increase right up to the point of full-blown stories when the children are older. The psychologist Susan Engel[13] has described a full range of developmental stages within story telling which reach up to the age of 12. In the young child they have a particular importance for the child's emergent sense of meaning. Understanding proceeds from placing experiences in a meaningful context and being able to identify with that context. Children also seek meaning in the thinking of the adult, which is one of the reasons they ask so many questions. If the activity or situation is meaningful for the adult, it will be much easier for the child to form his or her own meaningful relationship to it. This is especially true when the child's own sense of identity, of her own part in the situation, is in the foreground. Here we come to one of the great mysteries of early childhood. The child only fully understands something when she feels that her own understanding is confirmed by the adult.

The most important thing a child wants to understand is herself, and while this is egocentric, it is not egoistic. The child experiences the world as an extension of herself; thus, learning about the world is a kind of self-knowledge. The child wants the world to be confirmed, which means that she needs her view of it to be recognized and affirmed. This highlights the significance of shared meaning, of adults and children sharing an experience, putting it into words, not once but often, even telling other people about it. In this way the child feels part of a meaningful context, part of the story. The shared use of words, the retelling of the story, help form concepts which are still very personal in their colouring. This act of sharing experience and telling the tale is a fundamental one that retains its relevance in suitably modified form through childhood and right through life.

The talking about experiences forms the basis for thinking about them, and this in turn forms the basis for being able at a later stage to conceptualize. Children also do it on their own. As they play, as they lie in bed dropping off to sleep, as they sit strapped-in in the back of the car on journeys, they talk to themselves in a kind of train of consciousness, which can be interrupted to include new occurrences that can then be bedded into the flow. This external, audible speech gradually becomes internalized as thinking. Even as adults we do not entirely lose this ability to talk to ourselves in our own minds, and a surprising number of people talk to themselves when they are alone, or they write diaries and continue the inner dialogue with themselves in their minds or in words on paper.

A Treasure Trove of Words

The rich vein of insight we can gain from the anecdote about Mara is still not exhausted. The words themselves, when they are new and in context, are not merely symbols that represent something. At an age when activity, context, meaning, and sound are wholly integrated for the child, they become interesting, even magical things in their own right, to feel and hear, to roll on the tongue and taste. The phrase 'dicke Bohnen' in German is as real as the fat pale green beans themselves. It is not just an addition to the lexical list but a new treasure. The German word for vocabulary, *Wortschatz* (literally 'word treasure trove'), expresses something of this. In this way learning language *in context* (please note that we keep stressing context!) adds a dimension to a child's understanding of the world, and is not merely a symbol used as a practical tool. Something of the nature of the object is expressed in the word, in the way it is used. The more aware the adults are of the magical qualities of the words (for what we are describing is akin to what we call 'magic'), as well as the interesting qualities the objects themselves possess, the richer and more textured will be the child's understanding.

Names relate to their objects like garments. Different cultures dress differently because they *feel* differently. Each garment expresses something different about the object or concept they identify. In learning different words for the same concept we add different perspectives on it. In bilingual children, not only do words have different garments, but whole activities have a different feel because the structures that order them linguistically, the syntax, vary from language to language. Children appear to have no great difficulty acquiring more than one language simultaneously, as long as the adults are consistent and don't mix their languages. Children impose their own innate, emergent syntactical comprehension on what they hear.

The young child's hunger for meaning is the more easily nourished, the more *our own* understanding of the world is filled with meaning. Meaning is in this sense more than just a dictionary definition; it is a living picture of something that both values and integrates the many qualities intrinsic to the things around us. What is more, it brings those things into a relationship with ourselves. When this meaning is raised to consciousness and shared, real communication in the sense of communion, a uniting of self and world, occurs.

The Archetypal Qualities of Language

Language has three intrinsic qualities. Most obviously, it enables communication and the expression of our feelings and intentions. This aspect is apparent even at the pre-verbal stage of language development.

Secondly, and profoundly, language provides through its syntax certain structures that enable us to order the relationships we experience in the world. By defining the relationships between the subject (the doer), what the doer does, to whom or what, when, how, where, and sometimes why, language orders our experience of the world. All the relationships between people and things can be clarified through the structures of syntax, without which we would not be able to understand the world at all. In this sense the mental structures we use for thinking are the same we use to formulate our thoughts in speech. Moreover, something of the inherent order in the world of nature reveals itself to us through our syntactical thought structures. It is possible to use words without understanding the concepts behind them and it is possible to think without using words, but underlying both thinking and speaking are laws which are of a universal nature.

However, the third quality possessed by language is that words themselves, and words used in meaningful combination, reveal something of the *being* nature of the real and living world. In naming the world, the young child is not merely putting labels on his or her experience. The names possessed by things reveal something of their intrinsic qualities, not everything, otherwise all languages would use the same words, but something which, at least sometime in the origin of the word, was of meaning to that particular culture. When a child learns a word in association with a real experience, he or she acquires part possession of that object. In a real sense, through the word, something of the object becomes a part of the child and the child is united to the thing. The being of the object thereby comes to a higher form of expression through the being of the child. In religious terms one would call this a kind of redemption. In more normal terminology we would call this recognition. This may seem unduly philosophical, but when we consider the difference between oral and literate language it may become clearer.

In the next chapter we will attempt to focus this fascinating anthropological study on to the question, 'When is a child ready to read?'.

Main Points Again

- Communication involves more than simply the meanings of words or the obvious correspondence of gestures.
- Gesture is nonetheless a fundamental feature of human communication, together with body language and tone of voice.
- An experiment with pre-verbal communication...
- First the child stretches, then yells, then points, making eye-contact with mother and uttering intentional sounds.

- 'Proto' speech emerges via movement to identify objects and express demands.
- Healthy language development needs appropriate contexts and appropriately shared activities where meaning and intention is easy to read.
- 'Motherese', as distinct from baby-talk, is a distilled, concentrated form of language used in sympathetic communications.
- Learning language via motherese is not a graded simple-to-complex progression.
- Even if it is not the whole of the story, children clearly do imitate the language of their environment.
- Children focus on human speech and imitate the speaker's vocal movements even as they are listening to them.
- While imitation may explain the acquisition of accent and vocabulary, it is far less conclusively responsible for the learning of grammar.
- Three views obtain regarding the acquisition of language structure:
- The 'Nativist' view, which accords humans a language instinct;
- The 'Instructionist' view, which claims that language has to be learned from scratch;
- The 'Interactionist' view, which unites the two other views.
- Our own view would extend the interactionist picture to include the spiritual element of self-activity and the objective spiritual activity of language itself.
- Dialogue between child and mother begins before birth.
- Eye contact and voice recognition establish ground for continuing dialogue, which is a primary developmental need.
- Children need to be part of a real communicating community.
- The best advice to parents on supporting your child's language development.
- Neither baby-talk nor recorded speech offers healthy linguistic nourishment.
- Pre-verbal chattering naturally accompanies early activity as a monologue, which then expands into dialogues.

- A child needs to feel understood in her provisional experience of reality before she can fully understand it herself.
- Telling and retelling stories of shared experience gives a living meaning to words.
- Healthy dialogue also nourishes the ongoing monologue through which words help clarify thoughts.
- The individual words and the characteristic syntax of a language have life in themselves.
- Our communication with children needs to convey the feeling of a meaningful world.
- Language may communicate inner feelings and intentions.
- The inherent structures of grammar correspond to inherent structures in the world and enable us to make sense of them.
- Through language the world expresses its own inner being and potential as a direct communication to the human soul.

Practical Considerations

Here again, inertia is a main enemy of good practice. One way of dealing with it in ourselves is to undertake individual 'experiments' that don't threaten to overhaul our whole way of life. We might, for instance, experiment with learning and telling (not reading) a single story to our child/children – to see what it feels like. We might decide to tell another story drawn from the biography of our own childhood – to feel what is special about a personal communication in story form. We might decide to make up a little imaginative tale of our own – and surprise ourselves with the creative talent we didn't know we had! However much or little we do in this way will be enormously appreciated by our children, and should empower us to do more.

Consciousness is one of those words people use freely but find impossible to define. Its etymology provides some help. Derived from the Latin, con-sciere means 'to have knowledge together with someone else', which suggests that in its earliest stages, consciousness was actually a communal affair. A communal consciousness begins in orality, developing into an individuating, self-reflective activity only in literacy.

Barry Sanders, *A is for ox: the collapse of literacy and the rise of violence in an electronic age*, Vintage Books, New York, 1994

'Shall we have our milk now? That's a good boy. Have a good look round. What's that? Look there's your milk. Is that nice? Good boy. Yes, Mummy's got her glasses on. No, she didn't have them on before. Don't like them, do you?...'

Mother and baby aged 4 days,
BBC Radio 4, 1998

17. Ready to Read?

The whole issue of readiness is highlighted if we look at how and when a child learns to read. This is something that children clearly do need to learn, and many parents feel pressured to begin the process early.

It is of course *possible* to make a start with reading well before school age, and in many cases to achieve a respectable degree of literacy by the child's fifth year. But the question of whether a child is *ready* to read simply because she seems *able* to read is not nearly so straightforward. We need to know where the reading ability comes from, what other faculties are needed to support it, how fully developed these other faculties are, and how effectively they are able to contribute to the reading process itself. We need to know whether at a given age the activity of reading is consolidating other aspects of development or whether it may be taking something away from them. We also need to know whether the activity of reading (or indeed any other significant learning activity) may have the effect of actually *precipitating* other aspects of development – positively or otherwise.

In a book entitled *Orality and Literacy* by Walter J. Ong[14] we are given a powerfully persuasive account of how the development of writing and reading actually changes human consciousness. Oral or pre-literate cultures (a few of which still exist) are, he says, characterized in their thinking and expression by being 'empathetic', 'participatory', and 'situational.' The world is experienced not as something separate and inanimate, something we would label 'it', but as 'Thou', to use the philosopher Martin Buber's terminology. Literate cultures, by contrast, show thought and communication patterns which are 'objective', 'distanced', and 'abstract'. The literate mind experiences the world in terms of subject and object. The world is experienced as 'it', as object outside and apart from the self. The self is experienced in the oral mind through the experience of the other; a consciousness of self is always bound up with the perception of others, 'out there'. A literate mind experiences the self through itself, through reflection 'in here'.

A written communication puts a literal distance between writer and reader and denies the reader the immediacy of response available in a spoken conversation – including the often very eloquent but non-verbal human interchange that takes place when people speak with each other. The written word, and above all the printed word, also has the effect of making words appear like things: things that can be taken out of the flow of time and arranged and rearranged in space, for example in the form of a diagram or list, or in the poetry of e.e. cummings.

In the way that written language translates the oral/aural experience of spoken language into a visual experience, it also affects the way language is remembered and the way it informs our thinking. When we consider the ability of pre-literate cultures to remember hundreds and thousands of lines of their sagas and epics, we can be in no doubt that those cultures had a specific capacity for remembering words which we simply do not possess. We may also get the feeling that the inner experience of their sagas and epics lived on in those people in a way that ours, when we have read and closed our books, does not. On the other hand, of course, a literate culture can think, say, and do hundreds and thousands of things that an oral culture can't do.

Children, generation after generation, recapitulate what humanity as a whole has developed over the ages. In their early years they are 'pre-literate beings' with all the same qualities in their thinking and expression as pre-literate cultures. They are open to everything, involved in everything, and they register and remember what William Blake called the 'minute particulars' of their experience. A story told to a little child once needs to be told again in the same words if she is to experience it as the same story. And this is what she does want, again and again, because the continuity of her existence depends at this stage upon her experience being repeated rhythmically through the flow of time. Later she will naturally begin to detach herself from this need, just as human cultures have done and are still doing. She will come to *want* to develop a consciousness that is more independent of time, place, and circumstance – a consciousness that is more inward and her own.

This is the time when the experience of writing and reading will not only have its foundations fully in place, but will also bring what we could call a specific architectural stimulus to the 'higher' levels of human development. If it is introduced before the child is inwardly asking for it, then a new level of consciousness and capacity will indeed begin to arise, but it will be a house on shaky foundations and one that will not altogether feel like home.

No-one reading this book will want, any more than those writing it, to turn back the clock of history and see a wholesale return to cultural pre-literacy. But neither, surely, do we want to lose beyond recall the qualities that such a culture manifests. It is perfectly possible, if we allow the wisdom of experience to direct us, to have the best of both worlds: to enable the vitality of our 'childhood' condition to flow through and continually regenerate the more sophisticated condition that should grow out of it; and at the same time to become more consciously and individually aware of what it means to be alive, and of how we can make life better.

In a nutshell, the following points seem to us essential precursors (with the time they take to achieve) of a healthy and effective development of literacy:

- the development of listening and speaking skills through conversation, story telling, songs, and games where a clear and living language is of the essence;
- sharing many meaningful experiences with others, such as celebrating birthdays and seasonal festivals, where language is a medium of communion as well as simply communication;
- creative play with other children so that a real creative social interaction can take place, especially from the age of five onwards. (Children will delight in rediscovering such situations later as written about in books; they will also gain stimulus to continue such a living interaction and not simply to seek it vicariously through reading.);
- the cultivation of balance and fine motor skills through many practical activities, including domestic activities such as preparing food, baking, cleaning, and tidying up, gardening, crafts, and handwork skills such as sewing and using scissors;
- the sharing of a strong experience of structure, order, and rhythm in their lives as a basis for focus, attention, and application.

When the right time comes to make the transition into formal literacy it will still be important to preserve the sense of the word as a living experience. The following suggestions are based upon the practice in Steiner Waldorf schools, who begin this process only when the child is six:

- begin reading out of writing. The children should first write things they already know by heart so that their first reading is actually a process of recognition.

- before introducing the letters the children should have plenty of practice holding crayons and pencils and first moving and then drawing large clear shapes involving straight lines and curves, where the vertical, horizontal, and diagonal orientations are clearly distinguished.
- start with capital letters, which are easier to write and recognize. Evolve these letter shapes from pictures which embody their particular sound quality and which make them feel alive and not so abstract.
- let the children walk the letter forms on the ground, write them on each other's backs, model them in Plasticene and whatever else that can make them a physical rather than simply visual experience.
- keep the oral, imaginative, and pictorial element alive for as long as possible so that the children are able to form vivid inner pictures of what the written words represent.

In the next chapter we will examine the transition to formal education from a more general point of view. The reader is also referred to the Appendix on 'School Readiness', p. 000.

Main Points Again

- 'Readiness' involves more than just basic capability.
- The development of literacy skills needs to be fully supported by, and fully to support, other aspects of development.
- Distinctions between 'oral' and 'literate' cultures.
- The written word tends to separate, objectify, and generalize.
- Written words appear more like things.
- The experience of language shifts from voice and ear to eye and thought.
- Language is both experienced and remembered differently when written.

- Childhood naturally recapitulates pre-literate culture...
- and has a natural tendency to evolve beyond it at a certain time...
- ...which is when writing and reading become relevant.
- Orality and literacy should be mutually supportive.
- Some preconditions for a healthy literacy summarised.
- An appropriate transition to the formal learning of literacy skills summarized.

Practical Considerations

The measures suggested at the end of this chapter for preparing and introducing literacy have relevance for parents at home, even if their child has been or is going to be receiving a more accelerated course of instruction than we are recommending. The measures, which other books on Steiner Waldorf education explain in greater detail, may still have value as a kind of 'complementary medicine'.

18. The Transition to Explicit Learning

Jenny and Mark have two children, Elli aged 1$1/2$ and Tom aged 3$1/2$. They are debating whether to send Tom to nursery. 'Does he get enough stimulus at home?', they ask themselves. 'Does he get enough social interaction? A broad enough range of activities? Enough exposure to other adults who are 'good' with children, and who are qualified to prepare him for the life and work of school proper? If we don't send him now will he end up getting left behind?' 'But if he does start at nursery it will take him away from Elli and we won't feel like such a family any more. And maybe it will be too much for him anyway. Maybe he won't like it. Maybe it would make him grow up too quickly...'.

All the different aspects that Jenny and Mark are considering are relevant and potentially valid. Children *do* need stimulus, and by no means every home situation is an ideal setting on its own for providing this as children get older. The social interaction, the range of available activities, the qualified or experienced supervision of adults for whom this is a vocation, together with an environment devoted specifically to children – all this *could* provide a child like Tom with a better alternative to simply staying at home full-time.

From the point of view taken in this book, Jenny and Mark

will be fortunate if they have a Steiner Waldorf kindergarten in their area – or are willing and able to move to such an area. What a Steiner Waldorf kindergarten will *not* do is require Tom to be away from home all day, five days a week. This may be an available option, but not an expectation. As the teachers will explain to the parents at their initial interview, the kindergarten is there to support the child's experience of being at home, not to replace it.

The teachers will also clarify that the kindergarten will have much more to offer than simply childcare. It will indeed be a setting for formal education in the sense that it will actively promote specific features of child development. This will not, however, be through explicit instruction. To put it in the words used on the Steiner Waldorf Schools Fellowship's web site:

'Children's learning has a different character at each stage of development and for the child under seven the guiding principle is that of imitation. Steiner Waldorf Kindergartens provide a warm and loving environment where the child can follow the adult in activities such as baking, sewing, gardening, singing and painting. In a natural way the child is led into society and the world of nature by the example of the teacher.

All young children need to play and time is given each day for "creative play" where children can develop faculties appropriate to their age. In playing together, children learn how to act decisively. Play fosters social and interactive skills; in sharing and co-operating with others, the individual child begins to find his or her place in the Kindergarten family group and in the wider community.

Stories, verses, festivals and activities accompany the child throughout the year, marking the seasonal cycles. The earlier tradition, of telling well-loved fairy tales which deal imaginatively with the joys and sufferings of human life, is followed. These stories and traditional ring games – part of the culture of childhood for centuries – feature strongly in Kindergarten life, so that each child moves on to school with a wealth of songs and poems learnt "by heart".

Through such activities Kindergartens are places where rich experiences strengthen and fulfil the child and where enthusiasm for life and joy in learning are preserved and protected for the future.'

As the previously mentioned Channel 4 *Dispatches* programme[15] and the documentation of the research underpinning that report shows, other countries in Europe and elsewhere take the well-informed view that formal early learning is important, but exclude the introduction of reading and writing from that early learning. They place creative play as the key activity and see it as the means to educate the essential pre-requisites for effective formal learning, and create a basis for the reduction of socio-economic inequality. The Steiner Waldorf kindergartens across the world are established in a similar vein, although they have features that particularly distinguish them – notably the key significance given to learning through imitation, and the importance given to 'rhythmic' experience in its broadest sense.

If a Steiner Waldorf kindergarten is not an option there may still be other pre-school settings that seem reasonably child-friendly. After all, however, perhaps keeping one's children at home for longer will be the preferred solution – especially when it arises from the determination to meet the full spectrum of children's needs in whatever ways can be made possible. Parents should certainly feel empowered to consider this, however much pressure they may be put under to do otherwise.

The Transition from Implicit to Explicit Learning

If we have established a case for a non-academic form of early learning, then what does the child need from the age of six that he or she didn't need before that? What changes of emphasis are necessary?

The main change is one from implicit learning to explicit

learning. In the pre-school setting (kindergarten) the teachers have an agenda, they have learning outcomes that they are working toward, which essentially have to do with the child's physical development, habits, language skills, motor skills, and social and moral development. These are in many cases directed toward pre-literacy skills, such as listening and speaking through practice of articulation, retelling events in the child's daily life, story telling, reciting verses and rhymes, singing, and so on. The activities may be directed toward a number of developmental outcomes and the child's actual progress toward these ends can be monitored. However, the difference from explicit learning is in many ways obvious, but in other ways is actually quite difficult to recognize.

In explicit learning the child is clear that *she* needs to do the learning. She knows that her self-directed activity is called upon to be active, albeit largely in the context of an overall adult guidance. Before the age of around 6 years, the child's learning has been more or less unconscious and bound up with the organism and the senses. But now she has the first possibility (and it will still take several years for this to mature) of really focusing her thinking – for the basic reason that she can begin to form mental images not directly associated with sense impressions.

The transition from an early years approach to formal schooling should still retain much of what characterizes the child's way of experiencing the world and should remain pictorial, experiential, imaginative, related to an integrated whole picture, and above all interesting. What makes something interesting for a child is what she can identify with and what she can use.

If explicit learning is the task of education after the sixth year, then the child needs a learning environment that focuses attention and stimulates independent self-activity. Let us summarize such situations.

Each child has her desk and chair, her crayons, her recorder, and her book with her name on the front, and must learn to become responsible for these and other things. This process has been already begun in kindergarten (by having name labels on coat hooks, Easter plant pots, paintings etc.), but it is not a big focus. Now it should be. The child should feel: 'This is my place; it has been given to me by my teacher.'

In schools that have sensibly retained or returned to whole-class teaching, the children learn to do things all at the same time. Before school the child was quite capable of group activities but in a fairly informal way, and only for brief periods of time. The natural attention span is shorter and requires more variety. In pre-school, the children can and should move freely from one activity to another. Being able to sit quietly in a group and listen to instructions and explanations requires years of practice. Schooling depends to a very great degree on this ability being quickly established. In our experience, students and novice teachers have their greatest difficulties simply getting the children to pay attention long enough to catch their interest and kindle their enthusiasm for the task in hand.

Inability to concentrate is becoming increasingly typical of school age children, even those who have not been exposed to early formal learning. It has complex causes related to the environment we live in and over which we have relatively little control. The transition from a pre-school mode to school mode of learning therefore has to continue to work strongly with rhythm, varying the pace and focus as well as using elements of creative play which integrate the child's sense experience and engage their will in meaningful activity. Some schools have had positive experience of engaging children in practical activities before 'getting down' to school work proper. These might include going for a walk (since most have not walked far since they got out of bed), modelling, craft work, gardening, or domestic chores such as sweeping and cleaning. Music is also a great help, both singing and instrument playing.

Apart from their obvious readiness to listen to stories, pre-school children cannot be expected to sit still for any length of time and be instructed. Ordinary intellectual or prosaic language simply does not contain enough stimulation for young children's senses to follow, because their powers of visualizing what has been described are as yet undeveloped and unfocused. Story telling is different because the narrative structure and imagery are akin to the child's consciousness. Throughout the school age, in fact, children continue to learn best when the main content is in narrative form. This is true even with older pupils and students. The best science books tell *the story* of DNA or quantum theory. The old lecturing mode is unacceptable in many situations. We live in an age of dialogue, and many have neither the inclination nor the ability merely to listen for long periods.

With children in the younger school classes even instructions and explanations of an organizational nature benefit from some concession to pictorial imagery. 'We are going to walk quietly down to the hall like a herd going to water in the evening, not like a bunch of frisky foals just let out of the stables and not noisily like a flock of geese getting ready to migrate.' (Actually it might be better simply to stick with the quiet herd, since the images of the foals and the geese could prove altogether too evocative for some children to resist!)

Whole-class teaching is not only economical of time but enhances the feeling of individuality within the community. The children all face the same way, hear the same presentation, and see the same blackboard, and receive their tasks together. These tasks, however, are directed to individuals and will require conscious individual effort to fulfil them.

The teacher introduces the content of the lesson, then the children do whatever the appropriate steps are. The pre-school child cannot watch and then do, but has to accompany the adult immediately, inwardly if not always altogether outwardly. Of course this capacity does not disappear overnight, and one of the first tasks of the school teacher is to show the children that this is how they now have to work. 'I draw this straight line on the board. Now you close your eyes and imagine doing it. Now come to the blackboard and do it yourself.' This, in essence, is what the child needs in school. And whilst the forces of imitation remain in various forms, the primary shift of emphasis is from the children learning by imitating to their having the experience, internalizing it, and then directing their self-activity toward the activity in question.

Forgetting and Learning

There are many aspects of school teaching which support this primary activity, including the systematic and varied use of repetition and conscious recall. Experiences are allowed to mature through the night before being recalled the following day. This both strengthens the child's memory and also focuses the self-activity. This process of bringing consciousness to learning processes is crucial and of course has to be done in age-appropriate ways. The rhythm of experiencing, forgetting, recalling, articulating, applying, and then forgetting once more is vital to the learning process. The *forgetting* is really a shift of focus. If an experience has been strong enough and has made an impression, the child may stop thinking about it and go on to other things, but the experience remains – out of inner sight, as it were. It lives on in the body of formative forces which leave the trace of their activity in the neural networks of the brain.

In actively recalling the experience (and listening to others recall it from their perspective) and then putting it into her own words, the child learns to find a wider context for what she has experienced and this forms the basis for forming new concepts and understanding. Whereas the young child's memory has been situational and locational, the school age child's memory begins to become rhythmical. This means that sequences of related memories link on to each other, formed as it were into long loops by the regular repetition. This is called learning by heart, and lends itself to learning multiplication tables, verses and sequences of words, and the melody of songs. In a somewhat less conscious way, the spelling of words is also committed to memory. The next stage is to be able to recall isolated elements from the rhythm, out of context. Our experience shows that children increasingly need to retain visual or situational prompts before rhythmical memory becomes established.

Once a new skill has been learned through rhythmical practice, it can be allowed to sink down into permanent forgetting. As adults we fortunately cannot remember the long arduous stages we went through learning to read or skate with roller-skates. Now we have the ability and have happily forgotten the learning process. This highlights that forgetting, in this sense and most others, means not losing but placing in a deeper part of ourselves, indeed making it a part of ourselves.

Living Concepts

Learning reading, writing, and the notation of numbers and music are important aspects of making learning conscious. This learning must proceed from experience. Experience can be concrete or it can be in the form of language, but both have to be raised to conscious image in the child's mind. The image has to be flexible, capable of change and modification by new experience, and not merely a dry abstract concept. And concepts, when they are needed, should always arise from experience-based image, the more tangible and concrete the better, not least because this will weave in the child's emotional response and associations. This strengthens memory but also engages the will.

The Role of the Teacher

This picture aspect highlights the child's need for a different kind of relationship to her teacher. In the pre-school context the kindergarten teacher is a figure loved because she cares. This care manifests in the child's experience that everything has its place, that things are in order, that things are good (at least relative to everything else in a given environment). The teacher now needs to be a loving authority, an adult worthy of the children's respect.

Authority normally implies power. There is an authority that goes with rank, position, and role, and teachers have traditionally been seen (and have commonly behaved) like commanding officers. However, there is another kind of authority, which comes from the child knowing, 'My teacher knows'. This kind of authority cannot be enforced. It is the moral authority that comes with recognition and it is vital that the teacher can elicit this from the children, and also from the parents. This comes when the children intuitively recognize (and the parents observe) that their teacher knows them, loves them, and understands what they need in the way of guidance in order that they can learn, *and* that they are competent to create the right learning context. The healthy child expects, at first unconsciously but later with increasingly conscious recognition, that the teacher knows what to do. Children are very pragmatic and unsentimental about this. They ask, in effect, whether it is worthwhile to look up to this person.

Soul Food

This brings us to another aspect of formal schooling. If the first six to seven years have been primarily about providing the child with the right nourishment for their growing bodies, the second major phase of life is focused on feeding the mind or soul of the child. The stream of life needs to be directed to digesting information and converting it into knowledge. Just as in the first phase, nourishment has to be 'humanized', so too information has to be digestible. The child can most readily digest information in picture form, as an imagination. Dry facts, in this period, taste like ashes. Living images are like milk to the child's soul.

The role of the teacher in this is to 'pre-digest' complex phenomena to the extent that he or she can bring pictures to the child that the child can visualize, grasp, and understand, and which are also true to the nature of the subject. This places a heavy responsibility on educators: to have so immersed themselves in the subject and made it their own that they can have as a result the overview from which to bring the children the essentials. This must not, however, be too pre-digested or else the child's self-activity will not be stimulated (and that is not good news for the child or the teacher!). There must be a dynamic balance between nourishment and encouragement.

The Child and the World

One aspect of education has especially to do with *the child*, and has its focus in the development of skills and faculties. The other aspect has to do with knowing about *the world*. Both informal and formal learning should and always do involve the two aspects together. However, the emphasis in formal education has a tendency to shift much more in the direction of knowing and away from being. We do, after all, live in the 'information' age. The child is expected to learn a great deal of what is deemed to be relevant information, and also to be able to access it; and his or her skills are developed very much with this in mind. This is not the whole of the story, but nevertheless a significant part of it.

Of course children want to know about the world. They also want to know how to act in it. However, there is often a tension between the child's wants, abilities and needs, and what the world is asking from and offering to the child. Up to a point it would be fair to describe such discrepancies as part of the creative dynamic of education. Children do need to be stretched. They also need to be *prepared* for living in the real world. But they certainly don't need to be over-stretched, or deprived of all pleasure. Nor do they need to have their skills and faculties limited by adaptation to only a limited aspect of the real world, or frustrated because the world isn't asking for what they have to offer.

In the opening chapter of this book we referred to the phenomenon of children 'turning off' from education. We noted that this is becoming increasingly a feature amongst boys. How ironic this is, when the 'developed' world has set itself up so archetypally as a 'man's world'! The search for knowledge, the mastery of technique, the control of power: all these are acknowledged features of the male psyche. And it is today's girls who are growing up to inherit them.

In the next chapter we shall try to tease out this riddle more fully.

Main Points Again

- Particular early learning settings may have advantages over the 'home-only' situation.
- The Steiner Waldorf kindergartens have much to offer.
- Several European countries defer the teaching of literacy and numeracy in order to reap the extended and specific benefits of creative play.
- A summary of some of the special benefits of appropriate early years education.

- Some aspects of early education should indeed be formal; but this should be different from explicit intellectual instruction.
- When literacy and numeracy skills are introduced, this needs to be in a lively and relevant manner.
- Organic processes of growing and sensing govern the child's early learning, and the child needs 'weaning' from them carefully.
- The life quality and connectedness of experience should continue to inform primary education.
- Individuality is increasingly stamped into the furniture of the learning process.
- But individuality should nevertheless be experienced within the context of community and common expectations.
- Rhythmic and imaginative activity remains essential in the child's willing ability to concentrate.
- Telling stories is one of the best forms of instruction.
- Contrast between imitation and internalization of adult influence.
- Children need a rhythm of learning, forgetting, and remembering.
- Rhythmic memory replaces locational and associative memory.
- Skills, once rhythmically learned, can become unconscious faculties.
- Children need to be given mobile concepts anchored in life.
- The younger child's simple love of her teacher must now develop as a respect for her teacher's authority.
- Two kinds of authority, and the teacher's need to merit the authority of respect.
- As the child's body required healthy nourishment in the first seven years, so now, via the right kind of education, does her soul.
- The teacher must 'pre-digest' whatever subject matter is to be communicated.
- Current education processes tend to try and fit children to the world in a limiting way.
- A tension arises between child and world, which may or may not be creative.

Practical Considerations

As we said at the end of the last chapter, the absence of an ideal pre-school or school option is not the end of the world. A huge amount can still be done at home. There are also many evening and holiday activities that can complement formal schooling in a healthy way. Anything practical and artistic is especially relevant.

19. Do Boys Learn Differently from Girls?

Although there are significant differences between boys and girls, even in infancy, the differences between individuals are more obvious. Some babies are huge at birth, others tiny. Some babies sleep more than others, some have colic, some go through an extensive series of colds, coughs, skin irritations, and countless other torments (for parents too!), and some just sit there and beam back at the world like little Buddhas – regardless of their gender.

In general though, baby boys grow faster and become stronger and more active than baby girls. However, their fine motor co-ordination and language development actually lag behind that of girls. In fact, boys' brains develop more slowly altogether. Nobody knows why this is so and it is unclear whether it is a basic physical difference that is genetically pre-determined or the result of different experiences in their upbringing. It may be a result of both factors.

Boys may appear to be less sensitive but they can be more upset by changes of circumstances such as being separated from one parent or another. They can become very anxious and clinging. For this reason Steve Biddulph, the child psychologist and author of *Raising Boys*, advises against sending boys to day care or nursery before the age of three. They do much better if left with a relative or regular carer, if the parents have to leave them to go to work.

There is considerable evidence that the brains of boys and girls mature in subtly different ways. This has largely to do with the dominant proportion of the hormones testosterone and oestrogen, respectively, in the blood streams of boys and girls – girls have a high balance of oestrogen which stimulates the growth of nerve cells in the brain. The hemispheres of the brain grow at different rates in all babies, but in boys the left side grows even more slowly. This leads to an imbalance in the connections between left and right sides of the brain.

The human brain has a distinctive lateralization, and while the brain functions as an integrated whole, the different hemispheres are related to distinctive abilities.[16] In relation to literacy skills and early child development, the important fact is that complex skills such as those involved in reading and writing require good communication paths between the linguistic skills of the left hemisphere and the spatial and movement skills of the right side. The ability effectively to co-ordinate the perception of letters and words, or the motor control to write them, needs to be well connected to the perception of the flow of verbal language. Since girls' brains grow with fewer lateral differences than those of boys, the connections between the hemispheres are more comprehensive and thus the integration of the different cognitive skills is greater. With their somewhat lop-sided hemispheric development with the left side growing more slowly, boys have fewer direct connections between the two halves of the brain. Thus, the right side tends to have a greater wealth of internal connections, which may later express itself in a greater capacity for mathematical and spatial-geometrical thinking. The overall integration may, however, be weaker. In short, boys may frequently have difficulties with learning to read and write, communicate their feelings, and express themselves.

The lateralization of the brain only takes its final form around the fourth year in children of both sexes. That means that if one half of the brain is damaged, say during birth, up to the age of 4, the other half of the brain can take over the function. After the fourth year this is much more difficult. Women's brains, being better integrated anyway, have a better chance of compensating for damage, and women do, in fact, recover from strokes better than men.

All this argues for giving boys not only more time before teaching them to read and write, certainly after the age of six, but also argues that they should be taught differently (see below).

Whatever genetic factors there are, boys definitely become *more* different because of the way they are treated by their parents and other adults. Many people mistakenly assume that boys are more robust emotionally as well as physically and tend to treat them with less affection. They receive fewer cuddles and expressions of intimacy. Fathers, especially, tend to treat them as if they were older than they actually are and tend to wind them up more through rough play and excitement. Many fathers can't wait to engage their sons in manly pursuits such as wrestling, throwing, catching, or kicking balls (often half the child's size, such as soccer balls or American footballs), accompanied by boisterous and raucous calling, as on the training field. As Steve Biddulph wryly points out, if fathers had as little sleep as mothers, they might seek to calm boys down more than over-excite them before departing for the day to the office, leaving mum (or school, if mum works) to deal with the wreckage.

Sadly, boys also tend to get treated more harshly by stressed-out parents. They get smacked more frequently for misbehaving than girls. By systematically treating boys in this way, parents are unwittingly reinforcing behaviour patterns that manifest later in adolescence as anti-social behaviour, aggression, and over-defensive attitudes. Boys need to be treated with the same gentleness and nurturing care as girls. Furthermore they need to experience when they are young that men can be gentle and caring as well as strong and heroic, that men not only go out to work in cars but can also cook, do housework and gardening, read books, help children get dressed, and do the shopping.

Late Starters

As we stated above, one highly significant difference between boys and girls is that because of the slower rate of brain and linguistic development, boys are at a disadvantage if they are introduced to formal learning before the age of six to seven. In fact, even at that age they are still at a disadvantage, and it is crucial for parents and teachers to be aware of this. Considerable misery for all concerned can be created if boys are treated not merely as *different* but as in some way *deficient*. The fine motor control, eye/hand co-ordination and linguistic skills required as a basis for formal literacy have often not developed in boys before the age of seven. Let us remember that as beings with a four million year path of evolution behind us, the activities of reading and writing, sitting still in desks and so on are very recent and very unnatural. The fact that many girls can adapt to these challenges more easily than boys because of how their brains develop is not necessarily an argument that they should be introduced to literacy earlier.

Learning differences need to be understood, respected, and taken into account. The anxiety such problems can generate cannot be exaggerated, and the distress can be enormous. Boys who take longer to grasp the rudiments of literacy and formal numeracy can be psychologically scarred for life if they lose their self-respect and think of themselves as failures at the ages of six, seven, or eight.

There are powerful arguments (and no one has marshalled them better than Steve Biddulph) for boys not starting formal schooling until the age of six or seven, and even then they should go through school a year older than girls in their class. That means they would spend an extra year in kindergarten, where they would have time to develop the social skills they need and the fine-motor co-ordination.

This will be a difficult piece of advice for many parents and teachers because of the fear of being left behind in our highly competitive society, but the alternative is also worrying. Boys who have difficulties feel bad about it and typically experience failure. They notice that they are less competent and seek to compensate by refusing to take part so as to cover up their inadequacy. Their motor nerves are still growing and so they are continuously stimulated to move, and in a classroom situation this looks like disruptive behaviour. Stressed teachers trying to cope under pressure of attainment from parents and external expectations have no choice but to transfer the pressure to the child, thus escalating the downward spiral that leads to serious problems of de-motivation and alienation.

Of course not all boys have the same problems but enough do to make the situation worth addressing. There is much one can do to ameliorate the situation and give boys the support they need. Giving them more time to develop is the key.

We doubt, however that separating girls and boys is really the answer. The social benefits of learning together, even given the learning differences, is valuable enough in itself to justify fully engaging with the resulting challenges. There are many kinds of learning differences and not just those of gender. Integrating rather than separating children with learning differences is certainly harder for schools to cope with, and requires great flexibility on the part of the teachers. In the end, however, we believe the benefits in social perception, in mutual encounters and problem solving, in the cultivation of empathy through direct experience, through the aspect of learning through the (different) eyes of the other, outweigh the disadvantages. Whole-class teaching with undifferentiated groups of children has many social advantages, not least in providing children with a central role model as authority in the form of a teacher with overall and long-term responsibility for them. A class of children who have learned to appreciate the gifts of others in a direct and intuitive way will not need to be taught tolerance and respect at a later, more conscious age.

One key to making these nice ideas effective will be to hold back the start of formal education for boys and girls together. If the pre-school experience is appropriate, both sexes will gain from this. A second essential will be to develop same-age whole-class teaching in a way that accommodates and caters meaningfully for learning differences. Ways of evaluating these differences must be evolved that are not in themselves divisive and discouraging.

Main Points Again

- Boys grow faster than girls but develop more slowly.
- Boy babies and toddlers can be very insecure.
- Girls' brains are better integrated than those of boys.
- Boys are more likely to have problems with literacy.
- Boys tend to be treated more robustly, especially by their fathers.
- Boys need role models of men who are strong and caring and do housework.
- Boys are different but not deficient.
- Should boys start school a year later than girls?
- The long-term risks for boys under pressure of early learning.
- Learning differences are learning opportunities.
- All children benefit from a holistic and integrated approach.

Practical Considerations

Read Steve Biddulph's book *Raising Boys*!

20. Some Personal Experiences

The authors of this book have both being working within the Steiner Waldorf movement for some 21 years, and between us and our partners we have taught children from six to eighteen years of age. In this chapter we focus on how two pairs of children in our classes appear to have been influenced by their individual educational histories. We will look at a picture of children who have had only Steiner Waldorf education, and who in our view have experienced learning in harmony with individual development. We will compare this with a picture of two children who have begun in mainstream education as rising fives and then transferred to Steiner Waldorf education as eight year olds.

'Ellie' and 'Jon'

Both 'Ellie' and 'Jon' had older siblings in the Steiner Waldorf school and had been brought up in sympathy with the school's general ethos. They had been part of the Parent and Toddler group and then gone on through nursery and kindergarten until they were six. What they did there is indicated in general terms within this book, and is described in detail elsewhere in this series and in other literature connected with the education. Suffice it to say that they had developed a wealth of imaginative, linguistic, rhythmic, social, practical, and movement skills through their timetable of playful, artistic, and practical activities – without actually receiving explicit instruction in reading, writing, or arithmetic, or indeed anything much else besides, other than through good example and a carefully ordered provision of things to do.

During their final year in kindergarten both Jon and Ellie became harder work for their teachers, as did the other five year olds. They were definitely getting ready for something new. It was the teachers' challenge now to help them remain socially integrated within the group through extending their personal responsibilities for being helpful, and also to offer them more stimulating artistic and practical activities. In their final kindergarten term they had a special afternoon together each week with the peer group drawn from the school's different kindergartens who would go together into Class One.

Jon and Ellie know that in their last week of kindergarten they will be 'Jumping the Rope' to go into their new classroom and meet their new class teacher. They know that this moment will be as big as they come: it's going to be a real rope, and in their imagination it's going to take a BIG jump. As the time draws nearer they may be seen individually practising their jumps, focused and determined.

The moment comes. The door to the classroom and the corridor leading up to it have been garlanded with flowers by the children's parents. The parents themselves are lining the corridor, no less expectant and excited than their offspring. Ellie, Jon, and their classmates are led from the kindergarten by the oldest children in the school – for whom this is also a 'last week'. Further down the corridor they see the colourful 'rope' stretched across the passage at what is after all no more than shin height. One by one the children run and jump their individual rites of passage, to be born again as Class Oner's. Ellie gallops at the rope like an elfin horse, leaps it easily, and plunges straight into the classroom to be greeted by her new teacher. Jon has his eyes and mouth wide open as he runs, jumps – and then stands there on the far side of the rope in a long frozen moment of consummation. A parent gently turns him toward the classroom door, he realizes that the story goes on – and off he goes into it. The other children follow, gathering themselves together and then expressing their courage and resolution in a way they have never done before. There will be one or two who will need a little help along the way, but none will fail. They will remember this moment for life.

Inside the room, the teacher will have a little talk with them about what it means to be at school. The children will be asked about the sort of things their parents do, and the teacher will confirm how very capable such grown-ups are. Particular attention will be given to the clever things adults are able to do with their hands – because for Class Oners it will be the hands that learn before the heads. The children are told that in Class One they will learn to write. ('But we already can!', some say. 'Then you will learn to write beautifully', they are told.) The teacher further explains that the children will also be able to read what they write; that they will make their own books with lovely pictures as well as writing in; that they will learn to count up to some very big numbers and do clever sums with them – and much more besides.

The summer holidays go by. The first day of Class One proper arrives and Jon and Ellie get down to work with the children and teacher they will be staying with for the next eight years.

Every day in Class One begins with a Morning Verse spoken together by children and teacher, followed by a medley of singing, clapping, stamping, throwing and catching, rhyming, tongue-twisting, perhaps a little recorder playing and perhaps other kinds of 'body skills' activity as well. Then the main theme of the particular three- or four-week lesson block will be focused upon, involving a recall of what was learned yesterday, the new content of the day (at this stage often introduced via a story), and individual or group work arising out of learning that has been 'slept on'. After this two-hour lesson is over (and because of the rhythm of different activities within it, the time flies by) comes a short break. Between break and lunch come lessons like foreign languages, art, music, and other subjects where an element of continuous practice is essential. Then comes lunch, and after lunch the lesson which involves limbs more than head, such as crafts and games.

Jon and Ellie lap it all up. Their enthusiasm for almost everything appears boundless – although both have their own less favourite parts of the week, and always will have. Being so imaginatively and physically active keeps their cheeks a rosy red. From time to time they show signs of tiredness, perhaps even listlessness – but not long term. Their colourful, self-made 'form-drawing', writing, and numbers books give them pride and a real sense of achievement. Years later they will look back on these carefully preserved creations and retain a vivid memory of how the letter 'K' emerged from the picture of a king. They will laugh to see the occasional crown still left on the letter's head weeks after the picture had supposedly been left behind.

Both Ellie and Jon do indeed, as their teacher had promised, learn to read their own writing. The teacher had found it inappropriate to point out that they would actually know quite thoroughly what they were writing in the first place, and that their reading would initially be more a form of recognizing. The fact that it seems a real and exciting achievement to the children gives them the motivation and confidence to go on, and by the end of the year, with the ongoing visual recognition and phonics work that accompanies this literacy approach, they are beginning to read 'unseen'. Once started there will be no stopping them; and the same will be true of the majority of the class. Interestingly – and we can also say typically – neither child will need to wear spectacles while at school, even though poor eyesight has run in their families.

There are of course children in Steiner Waldorf schools who are slow learners, or who have special learning difficulties. Many though not all of these children have come into the schools after the kindergarten stage, having already been bruised by early exposure to the requirements of mainstream education. Through comparison with this latter category, there is no doubt in our minds that the Steiner Waldorf kindergarten children come to meet their learning challenges with a better foundation in terms of their pre-literacy and numeracy skills, with more vitality and imagination to apply to the task in hand, and with less background frustration and damage to their self-esteem than their mainstream counterparts. It may be that these children will nevertheless need to be offered some extra learning support after they have been through Class One, especially if they are significantly dyslexic. If so, this will be done as far as possible in direct relation to the work of the rest of the class. The class teacher will also take special care that the things such a child *can* do well are encouraged and celebrated within the class context.

Ellie and Jon happen to be at one of the Steiner Waldorf schools that finishes at Class 8. If they follow the path of their older siblings at that point they will transfer to Year 10 of a local comprehensive school. They, like their siblings and other Steiner pupils, will be openly welcomed there. The heads and heads of year have come to appreciate that these young people will bring with them an underlying enthusiasm and self-motivation in regard to learning itself; in general they will be less knocked off course than many of their peers by the negative aspects of the teenage subculture; they will be socially confident and self-confident, whilst also being adaptable. And they will pass their exams.

In Steiner Waldorf schools that continue to Class 11 or 12 the pupils also pass their exams – with a success rate above the national average. (This, it must be acknowledged, may reflect social as well as educational factors, since Steiner Waldorf parents tend to be very supportive of the educational process.) According to the Steiner Waldorf Schools Fellowship *Press Briefing* of March 2001, 'Results [of GCSE and A-level examinations] are around double the national average at 5 GCSEs Grades A-C'. In addition to their exam curriculum the pupils will also study more widely and freely than their mainstream counterparts, with all pupils continuing academic, artistic, and practical lessons. At the end of it all, they will go on to the things that young people go on to. No such extended study as the High/Scope Project (referred to in Chapter 2) has yet been carried out on the long-term after-effects of a Steiner Waldorf education, although significant research has been and is being done, including a study sponsored by the then West German Government (reproduced in Appendix 2, page 000) that was giving 85 per cent funding to their Waldorf schools. The available research clearly indicates that ex-pupils do go on to do well for themselves across a broad band of professions and vocations; that they tend to take a positive and creative view of their own lives; and that they are people with a social conscience. Usually their future work takes them well away from the 'Waldorf World' – until they have their own children, when, if they can, they commonly offer their offspring the education that was offered to them.

'Tim' and 'Clare'

Both 'Tim' and 'Clare' joined the school when they were eight, having previously had a normal English nursery and primary school education. Tim was academically very capable, while Clare was in many ways as bright as a button – but dyslexic with it. Both children had been brought to the school because their parents perceived that they were suffering constriction and frustration in their previous schooling.

Tim had some very individual quirks when he arrived. To some extent these truly were individual quirks – and he still has them four years on. In other respects the exaggerated nature of his behaviour appeared very much the product of being a sensitive child who had been driven too early into his head, by early schooling, by too much television and time on the computer, and by too little healthy food, fun, and fellowship.

He walked to and from school – slowly, with his back hunched and his head down. He hated to have to make eye contact with adults, and when asked a question would often completely refuse to speak. His desk was always a mess, he was forever losing things, and his work was clearly an embarrassment to him – maths was the only activity from which he seemed to gain any enjoyment. He held his pencil tightly, his writing was cramped and small, his drawings were empty cartoons, and any work with colour, though he was clearly drawn to it, seemed somehow like being asked to speak a foreign language. He would never sing or play music out loud with the rest of us, although something in him clearly wanted to; and it was the same with any form of movement. He made social connections within the class more quickly than he made any connection at all with his teachers, but even amongst his peers he was quick to take offence and clam up. His teacher composed a verse for him about a caterpillar hatching into a butterfly, to be learnt and recited each week in class. Because all the other children had their own verses to recite as well, Tim seemed to accept that there was no way out of it – and mumbled his verse (thoroughly learnt) in a barely audible monotone.

It is now four years on. Tim composes and recites his own verses these days. His poems are lyrical and 'deep'. He loves anything to do with drama, especially comedy. He sings and plays recorder. He loves painting, although it still frustrates him because he asks too much of it too soon. He's witty and popular. At the end of this school year, he even asked for a personal interview with his class teacher to review his year's work. 'I love interviews', he said. His teacher could hardly believe it; nor that Tim said he'd really enjoyed everything at school except German and Handwork. 'How about your teachers?' 'They're fine. Quite like some of them.'

Tim arrived in time – just – to rescue something that was vanishing from his childhood. He still spends a lot of time in his head, and his outlook on life has something of the 'Little Father Time' about it. But he's certainly 'more himself' these days, and his many talents are ripening and starting to feel much more 'sunny'.

Clare came with a face like early April – sunshine and squalls in quick succession. Her dyslexia had been confirmed before she came to us, and her parents felt she would be happier in a school where there would be less pressure on her. Already, however, she had developed an *I can't* attitude, despite having a powerful underlying will to develop and express herself, and to meet the world face to face.

Although unquestionably a colourful personality, she, like Tim, had a very muddled relation to real colours. She had no idea and couldn't see which two primary colours would make, say, orange. Nor could she keep to a rhythm. Nor sing in tune. Nor hear or create rhymes. Nor distinguish either aurally or orally between a significant number of different speech sounds. Nor read and write without the reversals and transpositions that typically accompany dyslexia.

Had Clare come to us earlier she would have had more

exposure to colour, rhythm, melody, the spoken word, including specifically chosen exercises (whether done consciously or through imitation) in listening and speaking, more work from Class One with the experience of symmetry – more experiences, generally, that would have helped strengthen the connections that were weak in her. This is not to say that all this would have cured her dyslexia – but it would surely have eased it, and better nourished and prepared her for the long challenge ahead.

As it was she did still come in good time. With some extra learning support, and with her particularly indomitable will, she has made the most of everything else on offer. Her colour sense is now wonderful, she sings publicly and 'a cappella' with a small group of girls from the school, she loves school itself, works hard at everything, and reads and writes for pleasure. Her dyslexia is still with her, and it makes reading and writing slow and still a bit hit and miss. But the stigma is gone, from the surface at least. It's a pity it ever had to be there at all, not merely because it hindered Clare's academic development but because her personal and social development suffered too. To some extent the shadow of this is still with her: her own determination to prove herself, mixed up with her deep-seated anxiety about 'messing', has left her still a little touchy at times.

****

We don't intend this chapter to be read as providing conclusive evidence that 'this is how it is'. We know wonderful, happy, and successful people of all ages who have never set foot in a Steiner Waldorf school, or been through anything other than a mainstream education. We also know of children – only a very few, actually – who have begun their education in a Steiner Waldorf school and never really settled into it. The justification for our chosen examples is that we feel they highlight the potential for education – especially early education – to bring either clouds or sunshine into children's lives. We also believe that the examples are typical in showing that the dampening of enthusiasm that may be associated with early education has the possibility of being redeemed through a more wholesome approach later on.

Dear Friends,

We, as a school, are so grateful to you for sending on to us such mature and charismatic boys and girls. I have commented before that our Steiner pupils bring an extra dimension to the school and it still remains a real feature of our school that there is a regular influx. Long may it continue!

Wishing you all continued success,

Mike Walmsley (Deputy Head, All Saints School, York)

---

21. Working Together as Parents and Educators

Successful individual development is never an end in itself. A fully developed person is also a social being. Social competence means recognizing the needs and gifts of others, and being ready and able to give and receive and find fulfilment in doing so.

The basis for social competence is trust. Its enemy is suspicion and lack of respect – however much this may appear justified in practice. Children bring with them an innate sense of trust in the world, and the adults around them become the custodians of this trust. Young children intuitively feel that, up to a certain point, the adult presence goes with them wherever they go, giving them security and a sense of orientation. The toddler in the park will explore within an increasing radius from the parent via a process of puppy-like roaming away and checking back. In crowded places like a shopping mall this takes a far more precarious form. Older children will stretch the invisible umbilical cord as far as it goes. At any age this cord *may* break. Getting lost is one of the most traumatic experiences a child can have. When children often experience a vacuum of adult presence and care, this can lead to a deep and permanent sense of isolation and alienation. One of the primary roles of the parent is thus to confirm and maintain the child's basic sense of security. A daunting task indeed – but fortunately one that most of us intuitively recognize.

When the child leaves home for school, 'home' must still be there to go back to at the end of the day. If the child cannot rely on this then everything done at school will be compromised to varying degrees – obviously. But the ongoing development of the child's 'social security' needs more than just stability at home. It needs stability at school and it needs the bridge between home and school to be open and trustworthy.

Traditionally the two roles of parent and educator have been rather clearly divided, and the school gate has represented this boundary. Yet we would not be the first to observe that the world has changed of late. On the one hand, the shape of families and the whole sense of 'home' has altered, with the loss of traditional family and community values. Coupled with this, the whole education system, especially in the western world, has had its foundations shaken. It is easy to see where this has involved a loss of something valuable, but in many ways it has also represented a liberation and opening up of new possibilities. At any rate both parenting and educating are having to find new forms; and the search for these new forms has to bring parents and educators closer together.

Already, in fact, parents have a more direct access to, and say in, what happens to their child at school. All too often, however, what drives parents to talk to teachers is a complaint. They know they have the 'right' to complain, and perhaps their motives for doing so are not always as considered and justified as they might be. Are they being over-protective? Over-ambitious on their child's behalf? Are they really in the picture regarding the realities of school life?

The teachers know the realities of school life better than anyone. These include being answerable to parents, governors, Government, each other, the children in their care, and their own consciences. Teachers are apparently the most 'stressed' of all professionals. No wonder, behind closed doors, they also bitterly complain.

All this is in the atmosphere our children breathe. Partly it is the product of an ill-ventilated and poorly illumined education system. Partly it is the product of a lack of social understanding, sympathy, and patience in the adults' communication process. In some cases it is simply due to individuals being unequal to their personal or professional responsibilities. Whatever it is, the children must inevitably inherit its consequences.

On the positive side there exist innumerable supportive parents and innumerable committed teachers who are united in their wish to do their best for the children whose interests they share. These are people willing to meet and learn from each other – about different ways of 'managing' children in different situations, and about the nature of children themselves.

How can such meetings be strengthened? We would suggest the following opportunities – none of which is a new idea, though rarely to be seen in practice all together:

- through schools inviting parents from time to time to see classes in action;
- through schools inviting parents to learn about and assist specifically in the teaching process;
- through parents offering an open door, on occasion, for teachers to visit their children at home;
- through individual discussions between teachers and parents where home and school perspectives can be shared;
- by having class parents'-evenings where teachers meet parents as a group to share and develop a collective picture of the class's work and progress;
- by having occasions where the whole school community meets together, for example in the celebration of seasonal festivals;

- by teachers and parents standing together against the inappropriate requirements placed upon schools from 'on high'.

Whatever the means we find to promote a better understanding and communication, the basis for success must be a common readiness to learn and develop – together. Surely the time is now ripe.

Main Points Again

- Self-development is bound up with social development.
- The basis for social development is trust.
- This is initially the prime responsibility of parents, then a responsibility shared between home and school.
- Discord between home and school may threaten the child's learning process.
- Positive bridge building between parents and teachers is essential, and can be furthered in a number of ways.

Practical Considerations

It is amazing what people can achieve simply through conviction and determination, especially when they do it together. The reader who has come this far through our book is encouraged to take heart: the world out there is willing and able to be made better. All sorts of people have the interests of children plus a lot of good sense in common. Our common error is to believe that the status quo is stronger than we are.

Conclusion

If our book is to have a conclusion at all we would like this to be, as T. S. Eliot put it in *The Four Quartets*, to arrive at where we started from and to know the place for the first time. We believe that there is a desperate need to remember – and at the same time to re-member – the humanity of our childhood. We do not believe that this is being nostalgic or sentimental. Enabling children to develop as children in the fullest sense is eminently practical, as well as a true deed of love. It will bring the best out of them, just as it will call to the best in us. The circumstances of our lives will in many cases make this difficult to achieve – but it will always be possible to make a beginning. What matters is that we have an interest in the question, that we are prepared to let go of our preconceptions and look at what is there, and that we believe in miracles when we see them.

Humanity tells itself a story of what human development and human learning is about. The story begins with a garden of innocence – fertile, fruitful, and full of life. Into this garden is transported a new-born 'creature of earth', whose first breath unites it in body and spirit with the world of nature and the creative power that sustains it. The garden provides both nourishment and interest for this human creature, whose first clear act of human consciousness is to 'name the animals' – to distinguish and identify the forms of life that surround it, just as a baby does with its first pointing and speaking.

Having distinguished itself from the animals, the original human being now begins to seek for its own reflection – just as a baby seeks in everything for a human face. Initially the discovery of 'another human being' is very much a continuation of what Piaget meant by 'egocentricity'. The Book of Genesis describes Adam communing with Eve as literally a part of himself. The distinctions of male or female don't come into it yet, nor those of self and world, nor of earth and heaven. 'God's children' carry on behaving like innocents, exploring and growing more aware of their world but not yet experiencing this as different from themselves.

The step into self-consciousness is a step into conscious duality. (The story divides Eve from Adam over the eating of the apple of *knowledge*.) Now the representatives of humankind become aware of their 'naked' difference. They become aware of what is good and not good, and what is God and not God. As the child does in its third year they feel the intimations of mortality. All this is symbolized in the story by their expulsion from the garden of innocence into a world in which they must *learn* to live and be at home.

Though God's children are no longer at one with God, there is still a clear sense of the divine presence at work in humanity's progress. God indeed still speaks to his children in dreams and appears to them in revelations within the world of nature. So, on the other hand, does the absence of God speak in nightmares and forebodings, and reveal itself as a barren wilderness and sense of homelessness. Every child on earth goes through this place of shadows. Every child's trust is tried, and feeling for goodness tested. There is only one desirable outcome for these tests – namely, that the child's trust and feeling for goodness is sustained and confirmed. Nothing can substitute for this. And nothing can bring it about unless there are human beings who care and ensure that it happens.

The process of 'the Fall' is a process of separation; the overcoming of the Fall is a process of trust. The Bible describes the original enemy of trust as knowledge, linking this with a kind of spiritual death. However, the same knowledge that drives Adam and Eve apart in the garden thrusts them together again in the world. As their story continues down the generations we see the development of a new kind of trust (continually challenged and frequently undermined) based not on innocence but on experience. This 'redemption'of the Fall is the conscious experience, not only of the ills of the world, but of the goodness of the world – enshrined above all in the goodness, indeed the godliness, of the human being.

Knowledge offers human beings choice and is the basis for human freedom. However, there is always something two-faced in the nature of knowledge: the same body of information can be used for good or evil ends, in both cases effectively and often, it might seem, with equally arguable justifications. What distinguishes a right from a wrong choice isn't knowledge by itself, but knowledge informed by a true feeling for life. This is what we may call moral knowledge. It is something more than blind faith, on the one hand, and blinding intelligence on the other.

Knowledge without a true feeling for life is – however well disguised – on the way to becoming deadly. Knowledge that *has* a true feeling for life – however naïve it may sometimes appear – bears within it the impulse of both wisdom and – dare we say it? – love.

The testaments of contemporary education are happy to speak of Knowledge and Capacity, but rarely if ever do they speak of Being or Love.

The reality of Being and the reality of Love are both the beginning and end of the kind of human education to which the effort of this book is dedicated. Knowledge of the world and the capacity to live and work in the world are a part of this; but the goal that encompasses everything, and the activity through which everything can be realized, is the Knowledge of Being and the Capacity for Love.

Resources

Worldwide Web Resources

The Steiner Waldorf Schools Fellowship (UK) has its web site at
www.steinerwaldorf.org.uk
(e-mail: mail@waldorf.compulink.co.uk)

The Alliance for Childhood (UK) web site is at
www.allianceforchildhood.org.uk
(e-mail: alliance@waldorf.compulink.co.uk)

The Alliance for Childhood (USA) web site is at
www.allianceforchildhood.org
(e-mail: jalmon@erols.com)

Building Peace Through Play has its website at
www.media-awareness.ca/eng/med/home/advoc/bptplay.htm

The Fair Play for Children web site is at
www.arunet.co.uk/fairplay/relate.htm
(e-mail: fairplay@arunet.co.uk)

The International Association for the Child's Right to Play web
site is at www.ncsu.edu/ipa (e-mail: ncsu.edu/ipa)

The Let the Children Play web site is at
www.letthechildrenplay.org.uk
(e-mail: info@letthechildrenplay.org.uk)

The Lion and the Lamb Project web site is at www.lionlamb.org
(e-mail: lionlamb.org)

The **National Children's Bureau and Children's Play Council**
has its web site at www.ncb.org.uk

The **Parentline Plus** web site is at www.parentlineplus.org.uk
(e-mail: centraloffice@parentlineplus.org.uk)

The **Save the Children** web site is at www.savethechildren.org

The **School of Storytelling** web site is at www.emerson.org.uk
(e-mail: mail@emerson.org.uk)

'**How Television Affects Your Child**':
www.kidshealth.org/parent/positive/family/tv_affects_child_p
rt.htm

TV-Turnoff Network has its web site at www.tvturnoff.org
(e-mail: email@tvturnoff.org)

The following online (all American) 'resource sites' bring together
Steiner Waldorf and home schooling, and include links to similar sites:

- www.bobnancy.com
- www.waldorfresources.com
- www.live-education.com w
- ww.oakmeadow.com

Contacts List

Steiner Waldorf and Anthroposophical Publishers

For names and addresses of publishers specializing in Anthroposophical and Steiner Waldorf education literature, and information
on the activities of the Anthroposophical Society, contact:

General Anthroposophical Society
Postfach 134
CH-4143 Dornach
Switzerland
Tel: (+41) 61 706 42 42 Fax (+41) 61 706 43 14
E-mail: sekretariat@goetheanum.ch

Waldorf Early Childhood Associations and Trainings

For addresses of national Steiner Waldorf early childhood associations, Waldorf early childhood teacher training courses and Waldorf early childhood centres world-wide, contact:

International Waldorf Kindergarten Association
   11 Heubergstrasse, D-70188
   Stuttgart, Germany
Australia
   Contact: Dr Renate Long-Breipohl
   44 Manor Road, Hornsby NSW 2077
   Tel: (+61) 02 9476 6222 Fax: (+61) 02 9940 3039
   E-mail: breipohl@smartchat.net.au
Germany
   International Waldorf Kindergarten Association
   D-70188 Stuttgart, Heubergstrasse 18, Germany
   Tel: (+49) 711 925 740 Fax: (+49) 711 925 747
   E-mail: Inter.Waldorf@t-online.de
New Zealand
   Contact: Marjorie Theyer
   c/o Kindergartern Training Course, Taruna College,
   Havelock North, Hawkes Bay, 33 Te Matu Peak Road
   Tel: (+64) 06 8777 174 Fax: (+64) 06 8777 014
South Africa
   Contact: Peter van Alphen
   c/o Centre for Creative Education
   PO Box 280, Plumstead 7801
   Tel: (+27) 21 7976 802 Fax: (+27) 21 7977 095
United Kingdom
   Steiner Waldorf Schools Fellowship
   Kidbrooke Park, Forest Row, East Sussex
   RH18 5JA, United Kingdom
   Tel: (+44) 01342 822115 Fax: (+44) 01342 826004

USA
Waldorf Early Years Childhood Association of North America
285 Hungry Hollow Road, Spring Valley, NY 10977
Tel: (+1) 914 352 1690 Fax: (+1) 914 352 1695

USA and Canada
Joan Almon
7303 Dartmouth Ave., College Park, MD 20741, USA
Tel: (+1) 301 699 9058 Fax (+1) 301 779 3272
E-mail: jalmon@erols.com

For a complete list of all Waldorf training courses and Waldorf
schools world-wide, contact:
Pedagogische am Goetheanum
Postfach 81
CH-4143 Dornach, Switzerland
Tel/Fax (+41) 61 706 4314

Other Useful Addresses

Alliance for Childhood
Brazil
Alianca para Infancia
Luiza Lameirao e Ute Craemer,
Av. Tomas de Souza 552, 05836-350 Sao Paulo
Tel: (+55) 11 585 15370 Fax: (+55) 11 585 11089
E-mail: ascmazul@amcham.co.br
Website: www.sab.org.br/monteazul
Germany
Alliance for Childhood
c/o International Waldorf Kindergarten Association
D-70188 Stuttgart, Heubergstrasse 18
Tel: (+49) 711 925740 Fax: (+49) 711 925747
E-mail: Inter.waldorf@t-online.de

South Africa
    Alliance for Childhood
    Jennifer Skillen and Yvonne Herring
    Greenhaus, 3 Eskol Lane, Constantia
    7800 Cape Town, RSA
    Tel/Fax (+27) 21 788 7867
    E-mail: childall@skillen.wcape.school.za
Sweden
    Alliance for Childhood
    Dragonvagen 13, S-177675 Jarfalla
    Tel/Fax: (+46) 85835 8516
    E-mail: sekretariatet@waldorf.se
United Kingdom
    The Alliance for Childhood,
    Kidbrooke Park, Forest Row, East Sussex RH18 5JA
    Tel: (+44) 01342 822 115
United States of America
    The Alliance for Childhood
    PO Box 444, College Park, MD 20741, USA
    Tel: (+1) 301 699 9058 Fax: (+1) 301 779 3272

Building Peace Through Play
    Ruth Taronno, Coordinator
    745 Westminster Ave., Winnipeg, Manitoba R3G 1A5
    Tel/Fax: (+1) 204 7758178

Fair Play for Children
    35 Lyon Street, Bognor Regis, West Sussex PO 21 1BW
    Tel/Fax: (+44) 01243 869922

Human Scale Education
    96 Carlingcott, Bath BA2 8AW
    Tel: (+44) 01275-332 516

International Association for the Child's Right to Play
Dr Marcy Guddemi
Dept of Education and Research
Kindercare, 2400 President's Drive
PO Box 2151, Montgomery, AL 36116 2151, USA
Tel: (+1) 334 2775090

International Save the Children Alliance
275-281 King Street
London, W6 9LZ
Tel: (+44) 020 87482554 Fax: (+44) 020 82378000
E-mail: info@save-children-alliance.org

Let the Children Play
Hillview, Portway Hill, Lamyatt
Shepton Mallet, Somerset BA4 6NJ
Tel: (+44) 01749-813 260 or 01749-813 971

Montessori Society AMI UK
6 Lyndhurst Garden
London NW3 5NW
Tel: (+44) 020 7435 7874 Fax: (+44) 020 7431 8096

The National Children's Bureau and Children's Play Council
8 Wakley Street, London EC1V 7QE
Tel: (+44) 020 78436000 Fax: (+44) 020 72789512

National Playing Fields Association
Stanley House, St. Chad's Place
London WC1X 9HH
Tel: (+44) 020 78335360 Fax: (+44) 020 78335365
E-mail: npfa.co.uk

Parentline Plus

520 Highgate Studios, 53-59 Highgate Road
Kentish Town, London NW5 1TL
Tel: (+44) 020 7204 5500 Fax: (+44) 020 7284 5501
Helpline: (+44) 0808 800 2222

School of Storytelling

Emerson College, Forest Row, East Sussex RH18 5JX
Tel: (+44) 01342-822 238

The Lion and the Lamb Project

4300 Montgomery Avenue – Suite 104
Bethesda, Maryland 20814, USA
Tel: (+1) 301 654 3091 Fax: (+1) 301 654 2921

The Early Years Trainers Anti Racist Network

PO Box 28, Wallasey CH45 9NP
Tel/Fax: (+44) 01516 396136

The Working Group Against Racism in Children's Resources

460 Wandsworth Road, London SW8 3LK
Tel: (+44) 020 76274594

TV-Turnoff Network

1601 Connecticut Avenue, NW 303
Washington, DC 20009 USA
Tel: (+1) 202 5185556 Fax: (+1) 202 5185560

World List of Rudolf Steiner Waldorf School Associations

The full list of kindergartens, schools and training courses, together with information for countries not listed below (running to some 80 pages in all), can be obtained from:

The Pedagogical Section of the School of Spiritual Science
Goetheanum
CH-4143 Dornach, Switzerland

Full title: *World List of Rudolf Steiner (Waldorf) Schools and Teacher Training Centers, Stand Februar 2000*, Herausgegeben vom Bund der Freien Waldorfschulen e.V., Heidehofstrasse 32, D-70184, Stuttgart (Tel. ++49 (0)711-21042-0; e-mail bund@waldorfschule.de)

With thanks to the publisher for permission to reproduce this (abbreviated) list; and to the editor of the journal Steiner Education, Dr Brien Masters, for permission to use that journal's list summary.

Australia
Association of Rudolf Steiner Schools in Australia
213 Wonga Road, Warranwood, Victoria, Australia, 3134

Austria
Österreichische Vereinigung freier Bildungsstätten auf anthroposophischer Grundlage
Endresstrasse 100, A-1230 Wien

Belgium
Federatie van Rudolf Steinerscholen in Vlaanderen
Kasteellaan 54, B-9000 Gent

Canada
Association of Waldorf Schools of North America
c/o David Alsop, 3911 Bannister Road, Fair Oaks
CA 95628, USA

Ontario: Waldorf School Association of Ontario
9100 Bathurst Street, Thornhill
Ontario L4J 8CF, Canada

Denmark
Sammenslatningen af Rudolf Steiner Skoler i Denmark
Strandvejen 102, DK-8000 Arhus

Estonia
Eesti Waldorfkoolide Uhendus
14 Koidula Tanav, EE2100, Rakvere, Estonia

Finland
Steinerpedagogiikan seura ry-Foreningen- for Steinerpedagogik rf
c/o Lea Blafield, Jyvaskylan Rudolf-Steiner-koulu
Honka harjuntie 6, FIN 40600 Jyvaskyla

France
Fédération des Écoles Rudolf Steiner en France
11 rue de Villaines, F-091370 Verrières-le-Buisson

Germany
Bund der Freien Waldorfschulen e.V.
D-70184 Stuttgart, Heidehofstrasse 32

Ireland
Irish Steiner Waldorf Education Association
Raheen Road, Tuamgraney, County Clare

Italy
Associazone Amici Scuola, via Clerici 12
1-22030 Camnage Volta (COMO)

Latvia
Lettishe Assoziation fur Waldorf-padagogik
Pirma iela 26a, Rigarajons, LV 2164

Luxembourg
Verain fir Waldorfpadagogik Letzebuerg
45 Rue de l'Avenir, L 1147 Luxembourg

Netherlands
    Bond van Vrije Scholen
    Hoofdstraat 14 B, NL-3972 LA Driebergen
New Zealand
    Federation of Rudolf Steiner Schools
    PO Box 888, Hastings, Hawke's Bay
Norway
    Steinerskolene i Norge
    Prof. Dahlsgt. 30, N-0260 Oslo
Romania
    Federatia Waldorf din Romania
    Bd.Marasti nr.59, sector 1, RO-71331 Bucuresti
Slovenia
    Drustvo prijateljev, waldorfike sole
    Rodiceva 2,61000 Ljubljana, Slovenia
South Africa
    Southern African Federation of Waldorf Schools
    PO Box 67587, Bryanston, Transvaal, 2021 Johannesburg
Sweden
    Waldorfskolefederationen
    Fridhemsgatan 17, S-12240 Stockholm
Switzerland
    Koordinationsstelle der Rudolf Steiner Schulen in der Schweiz
    Robert Thomas, Carmenstrasse 49, CH-8032 Zürich
United Kingdom
    Steiner Waldorf Schools Fellowship
    Kidbrooke Park, Forest Row, East Sussex RH18 5JA
USA
    Association of Waldorf Schools of North America
    Chairman, 3911 Bannister Road, Fair Oaks, CA 95628

Notes

1   Caroline Sharp, paper prepared for the NFER's Annual Conference, Great George Street Conference Centre, London, Tuesday 6 October 1998,
http://www.nfer.ac.uk/conferences/earlybib.htm#international

2   We have opted in this book to use feminine pronouns when referring to the 'generalized child'. This is partly to avoid the often cumbersome 'his or her' alternative. It is also to try and encourage the reader to look at childhood in a new way. However, please be aware that any picture of a 'generalized child' very quickly becomes an abstraction; in particular it is wholly inappropriate to think that *his* and *her* mean the same thing in reality. We shall be looking at the differences between boys and girls later.

3   The emphasis here is on 'meaningfully'. Often children will use the first-person pronouns out of imitation, without this being a true ego experience, before the real nodal point of self-consciousness is reached.

4   Where breast-feeding is not possible, for whatever reason, the next crucial priority is intimate contact. Human beings are immensely adaptable, and can and do cope with all manner of deprivations, including being deprived of mother's milk. Our point is that breast-feeding is best when it is possible, not that it is essential.

5   Quoted from an interview with Joseph Chilton Pearce in *Wild Duck Review*. Pearce also describes these phenomena in

his books *Evolution's End* (Harper San Francisco, October 1993) and *Magical Child* (Plume, March 1996). Quoted in the transcript of the 'Horizon' Programme *The Man who Made up His Mind*, transmitted 24 January 1994, BBC Education.

6   Quoted in the transcript of the 'Horizon' Programme *The Man who Made up His Mind*, ibid.

7   See J. Healy, *Failure to Connect*, Simon and Schuster, New York, 1999. The quotation is taken from an article by Emma Haughton in *The Independent*, 3 June 1999, 'Look what they've done to my brain, ma'.

8   B. Cyrulink, *The Dawn of Meaning*, McGraw Hill, New York, 1993.

9   Quoted in R.F. Cromer, *Language and Thought in Normal and Handicapped Children*, Blackwell, Oxford, 1990, p. 197.

10 W.S. Condon and W.D. Ogston, 'Speech and body motion synchrony of the speaker-hearer', in D.H. Horton and J.J. Jenkins (eds), *Perception of Language*, Columbus, Ohio, 1971, pp. 150-73.

11 See S. Pinker, *The Language Instinct*, Penguin, Harmondsworth, 1994.

12 See G. Wells, *The Meaning Makers*, Heinemann, Portsmouth, NH, 1987; J. Bruner, *Child's Talk: Learning to Use Language*, Norton, New York, 1983; L.S. Vygotsky, *Mind in Society*, Harvard University Press, Cambridge, Mass., 1978.

13 S. Engel, *The Stories Children Tell*, W.H. Freeman, Basingstoke, 1994.

14 Walter J. Ong, *Orality and Literacy: The Technologizing of the Word*, Methuen, London and New York, 1982.

15 *Dispatches: 'The Early Years'* by Clare and David Mills (see Chapter 1).

16 See R.F. Schmidt and G. Thews, *Human Physiology* (Chapter 10.1, Cerebral Asymmetry), Springer-Verlag, Berlin, Heidelberg and New York, 1989.

Bibliography

R. Baldwin-Dancy, *You are your child's first teacher*, Celestial Arts, Berkeley, 2000 (orig. 1989).

S. Biddulph, *Raising boys*, Thorsons/HarperCollins, London, 1998 (orig. 1997).

T. Bruce, *Time to play – in early childhood education*, Hodder and Stoughton, London, 1992.

C. Coordes & E. Miller, *Fool's gold: a critical look at computers in childhood*, Alliance for Childhood, Forest Row, Sussex, 2000.

S. Engel, *The stories children tell: making sense of the narratives of childhood*, W.H. Freeman, London, 1995.

M. Glöckler, & W. Goebel, *A guide to child health*, Floris Books, Edinburgh, 1990.

F. Jaffke, *Work and play in early childhood*, Floris Books, Edinburgh, 2000.

S. Jenkinson, *The Genius of Play*, Hawthorn Press, Stroud, 2001.

I. Haller, *How children play*, Floris Books, Edinburgh, 1991.

J.M. Healy, *Failure to connect: how computers affect our children's minds – for better and worse*, Simon and Schuster, New York, 1998.

H. Heckmann, *Nøkken, a garden for children*, Waldorf Early Childhood Association/Association of Waldorf Schools of North America, 2000.

B.C.J. Lievegoed, *Phases of childhood*, Floris Books, Edinburgh, 1987.

L. Miller et al., *Closely observed infants*, Duckworth, London, 1989.

L. Oldfield, *Free to Learn: Introducing Steiner Waldorf Early Childhood Education*, Hawthorn Press, Stroud, 2001.

V. G. Paley, *Wally's stories – conversations in the kindergarten*, Harvard University Press, Baltimore, 1981.

B.J. Patterson. & P. Bradley, *Beyond the rainbow bridge: nurturing children from birth to seven*, Michaelmas Press, Amesbury, Mass., 2000.

L. Purvis, & S. Selleck, *Tuning in to children – understanding a child's development from birth to 5 years*, BBC Education, London, 1999.

M. Rawson, *Free your child's true potential*, Hodder & Stoughton, London, 2001.

M. Rawson (ed), *Guidelines to School Readiness*, Pedagogical Section, Steiner Schools Fellowship Publications, Forest Row, Sussex, 2001.

M. Rawson & T. Richter, *The educational tasks and content of the Steiner Waldorf curriculum*, Steiner Schools Fellowship Publications, Forest Row, Sussex, 2000.

J. Salter, *The Incarnating Child*, Hawthorn Press, Stroud, 1987.

D.E. Stern, *Diary of a baby: what your child sees, feels and experiences*, HarperCollins, London, 1990.

M. Strauss, *Understanding children's drawings*, Rudolf Steiner Press, London, 1978.

J.B. Thompson (ed.), *Natural childhood: a practical guide to the first seven years*, Gaia Books, London, 1994.

ALPHABET DRAWINGS

DESIGNED AND
DRAWN BY
TOM NEIL
CLASS ONE
TEACHER
RUDOLF
STEINER
SCHOOL
SOUTH DEVON
1995 · 6

Appendix 1: School Readiness

In Waldorf education the seven-year developmental cycle is considered to be a great support for the child's own maturation. For this reason children are introduced to formal learning in Class 1 during their seventh year. Ideally this applies to all children. There is no selection process. Internationally the cut-off date for Class 1 readiness is considered to lie around 30 May for children starting school in August/September. That is to say, children should have had their sixth birthday before that date. A month either side of this date is considered borderline. The following criteria for school readiness are not intended as selective criteria but rather as guidelines for assessing the child's developmental stage. Many professionals, including teachers, child psychologists, and school doctors, consider that keeping children of the appropriate age for school entry back for a year can, in the long run, do as much harm as can premature entry to formal schooling.

The issue of social inclusion is relevant here. It is generally considered that Waldorf education should be available to all children. It is up to the school to assess each child's needs and develop an individual education plan to meet each child's needs. Obviously this is also a question of resources and training as to whether the school can actually offer adequate provision for all children. Nevertheless, the principle is clear: Waldorf education strives, in principle, to meet every child's needs.

In Europe some larger Waldorf schools are experimenting with a Summer Class 1 and a Winter Class 1, the latter being for children who would be very young in their class or who, for other reasons, need more time to develop. The Winter Class 1 may start in December or January, and this class would catch up with their parallel class by the start of Class 2 (a fact that shows that the Waldorf curriculum is not a matter of quantity of content in each year but rather of development through the curriculum). At the same time, many early-years settings, in partnership with schools, are developing new approaches for offering the kindergarten's rising six year olds more activities designed to help with their transition to formal schooling. The reason behind this is the recognition that the changing social and environmental context means that many children are simply not able to develop to the point of 'readiness' within the first six years. In fact, one experienced school doctor advised recently that most children were in fact 'unready' for school even at the appropriate age, and that unreadiness should be considered normal for Class 1. If this proved to be typical, it would have consequences for teaching methods in the first primary class. Far more focus would have to be made on helping bring 'readiness' about. The distinction between implicit and explicit teaching/learning would remain the guiding principle, since it is the method that counts more than the content – that is, how something is done rather than what is done.

The view we are putting forward in this book is that the way children learn is part of the overall way children develop. The times when children are ready to learn in new ways are, equally, nodal points in their general development. Child development is certainly not a mechanical affair, but neither is it arbitrary. It is the reflection of fundamental processes that are inherently consistent and predictable. Developmental differences between children are significant, but they do not imply that there are different developmental laws.

The most important fact about child development is that it is holistic. Physical, emotional, and intellectual aspects of a child's nature are profoundly linked, reflecting and affecting each other in ways that can be, and are being, established scientifically. Whilst this scientific confirmation is especially important in the face of current misconceptions, it is also important to realize that developmental realities may also be confirmed by consistent observation and common sense.

The following 'developmental check-list' is drawn largely from guidelines in use amongst the Steiner Waldorf schools to help form the picture of when a child is felt to be ready to move from kindergarten to their first class – generally in their sixth or seventh year. The check-list belongs to a tried and tested educational practice: a practice that is closer to the 'Central European' than the 'English' model, although one with distinctive features of its own. *We must emphasize that neither we nor the Steiner Waldorf schools would wish this list to be seen as a score sheet where so many ticks here or there imply a definite decision about a child's school readiness.* It is used in the schools as a set of notes to support a genuine and open discussion between parents and teachers as to what is really right for a particular child.

Developmental principles are a reality. So is individuality.

A Checklist for School Readiness

Physical Development

Certain anatomical features show that overall physical growth and development are normal for the age. A certain physiological readiness in terms of co-ordination, fine and gross motor skills, and balance is necessary if children are to start with formal literacy. Indications that the child has difficulties in areas of motor co-ordination are important to note. If all other indications point to the fact that the child is otherwise ready, then some remedial support can be given to strengthen motor skills and co-ordination. The anatomical features are general indicators of physical maturity. The school-ready child normally shows:

- visible knuckle joints and kneecaps in place of dimples;
- arch in the foot;
- individualized facial features instead of baby features;
- S-curve in spine;
- evidence that second dentition has begun;

and can typically

- touch top of ear by reaching over top of head with opposite arm;
- walk forward on a beam, log, or line;
- catch and throw a large ball;
- hop on either foot;
- bunny hop (both feet together);
- habitually walk in cross pattern (i.e. swing opposite arm when stepping out with one foot);
- climb (but not necessarily descend) stairs with alternating feet on each stair;
- tie knots or, sometimes, bows; button/zip own clothing;
- use fingers dextrously (sew, finger knit, play finger games etc.);
- demonstrate established dominance (especially eye/hand laterality)

– although in some cases this may not be apparent before around 9 years; and

- shake hands with thumb separated from fingers, rather than offering the whole hand.

Social/Emotional Development

As indicators of typical developmental progress the following summary may be helpful. The pre-school stages are characterized by:

- *Age 3:* not really social with other children; wants to possess things and try them out; reactive, transitory feelings, quick mood changes;
- *Age 3-4:* begins to discover the 'other person', but still essentially self-centred;
- *Age 5:* real need for social experience; beginning of give-and-take, sharing; some beginnings of joint planning in play.

The school-ready child develops (or with encouragement can develop):

- a feeling for others' needs;
- the beginnings of deeper friendships;
- a growing awareness of the principle of authority, e.g. as evidenced in games of animals and their owners;
- the ability to visualize objects or suggested situations;
- the ability to be more self-contained in his or her inner life;
- the ability to join in offered activities;
- the ability to look after his or her own eating, drinking, washing, and toileting needs;
- the ability to share a teacher's or parent's attention and wait for a turn;
- the ability to follow instructions and carry through a task or activity; and
- the ability not be unduly dependent on a 'security item' (thumb, blanket etc.).

Drawing and Painting

Children's drawings and paintings reveal their developmental progression. The pre-school stages can characterized as follows:

- *1st stage:* all about movement and process – forms and motifs appearing out of movement but are not the child's focus in the activity;

- *2nd stage:* the emergence of fantasy – the child begins to identify objects as they appear in the process of drawing rather than deliberately setting out to draw or paint them; also happy simply to play with the flow of colour;
- *3rd stage:* evolution of complete human form, including the use of the triangle; more interest in colouring in.

The school-ready child:

- will produce two-fold symmetries in free drawing, indicating the establishment of the brain's hemispheric functioning;
- draws 'change of teeth' pictures, containing horizontal repetitions such as birds flying, rows of mountains, castle crenellations, etc. reminiscent of rows of teeth;
- distinguishes strips of earth and sky, showing awareness of 'above and below' in contrast to the young child's feeling of wholeness;
- use of diagonal (related to perspective) – this is frequently seen in the triangle form of a roof or in drawing of stairs; and
- people, houses, trees, etc. rest on the grass or ground near the bottom of the page.

Development of Intention

The child's will development can be characterized as follows. The school-ready child:

- shows conscious goals in his or her activity;
- shows growing awareness of (and often frustration at) the distinction between inner intention and outer result – 'I can't do it';
- shows signs of being dissatisfied, not knowing what to do with themselves – often expressed as 'I'm bored'; and
- enjoys vigorous limb activities; likes to run errands (showing both goal consciousness and a new sense of authority).

Development of Inner Feeling

The school-ready child:

- shows signs of being able to manage his or her own feelings;
- likes to wrap objects as gifts for specific people;
- loves humour, limericks, rhymes, play on words, silly words, naughty words, showing a new consciousness for language and its power;

- shows conscious awareness of rhythm;
- likes to whisper and have secrets (distinction between inner and outer); and
- may like to tell of dreams.

Development of Thinking

The school-ready child:
- has begun to develop simple causal thinking in relation to concrete situations ('if', 'because', 'therefore'- for example; 'If I tie these strings together, they will reach that door');
- enjoys literally tying things together with string etc.;
- shows better use of verb tenses, e.g. 'I stood', not 'I standed';
- enjoys cunning, planning, scheming;
- enjoys riddles;
- shows an ability to access memories consciously on request;
- speaks clearly and fluently when relaxed;
- can concentrate on a chosen task for 10-15 minutes;
- can visualize things inwardly on request and can describe them; and
- begins to ask 'real' questions (not the typical younger child's constant 'why' for the sake of asking it).

Please note: It is generally the case that at this stage of development, boys are about 6 months behind the girls.

What we can say is that a later start appears not to be a disadvantage to children's progress (although it is important not to forget the important contribution made by children's experiences at home and in pre-school). Certainly, there would appear to be no compelling educational rationale for a statutory school age of five or for the practice of admitting four-year-olds to school reception classes.

Caroline Sharp, private paper prepared at Ofsted's request for the NFER's (National Foundation for Educational Research) Annual Conference, October 1998

Children should not start formal lessons until the age of seven, teachers said today. Members of the Association of Teachers and Lecturers called for classes in the three Rs to be delayed up to two years in schools, with children left largely to play instead of starting at five as at present. Delegates claimed children were being damaged by the Government's insistence on formal instruction in writing, reading and basic sums in nurseries and reception classes. Many pupils – particularly boys – who develop more slowly than girls – are incapable of coping with English and maths at five and feel 'failures' when they can't keep up, it was suggested. They are put under intolerable pressure by 'pushy' parents who 'cram' them with information and hire tutors to ensure they pass national tests, it was claimed. Early success for children had become a 'status symbol' among many middle class parents.

Tony Haplin, Education correspondent, *Daily Mail*
Thursday 1 April 1999

Children are being forced into formal lessons at too young an age, a committee of MPs warned yesterday. They said the Government's focus on literacy and numeracy could damage the education of the under-fives. In a report, the Commons Education Select Committee also said children were being forced to start school too soon. It urged the Government to review the financial pressures that force schools to enrol as many four-year-olds as possible, and pressure on parents to take a place at a chosen school as soon it comes up. Barry Sheerman, committee chairman, said: 'We don't want to see very young children sitting in classes of 30 being taught by one member of staff in a regimented way.' They had seen a class of three-year-olds with one teacher tracing letters of the alphabet, he said. The report says the adult:child ratio should be one to 15 in the first two years. Children starting school at four today may be in classes of 30. A spokesman for the Department for Education and Employment said: 'There is no way we want kids to sit in rows. They should be learning through play. But we don't think it is too early for children to start developing the skills they need for later educational development.'

Judith Judd, 'MPs warn children are taught too soon', Education Editor, *The Independent* newspaper, Friday 12 January 2001

Appendix 2: Research on Waldorf School Graduates

Excerpts from an article in *Der Spiegel*, 14 December 1981

[Explanatory Note: *Der Spiegel* is a German weekly news magazine, somewhat analogous to the English-language *Time* or *Newsweek* magazines.]

Waldorf Schools, generally reputed to produce 'beautiful souls' weakened for the tasks of real life, actually do quite the opposite, say results of a study which could even correct the evaluation of *Gesamtschulen* (twelve-year schools which include both those students preparing for college and others as well).

During the current school year, 32,000 students are being educated outside the state school system in 72 Free Waldorf Schools – according to the pedagogical concepts of the anthroposophist Rudolf Steiner. They attend a school which, according to the aims of their founder, aspires to transmit not only knowledge and ability but also content helpful for life and a perspective on life's purposes. Their school day does not follow the 45-minute beat of strict timetables, but runs according to the rhythm of 'blocks' and, during the first eight years, with strong artistic emphasis. Their career is not accompanied, year after year, by reports, marks and promotions, but is free of selection[1] and pressures of grading – a tempting perspective surely, but for many parents hardly a realistic one or an adequate preparation for the battles of life.

This view is now being shaken by a scientific study of 'The Educational Background of Former Waldorf Students' – the first empirical research of the Waldorf movement.

Three independent scientists, paid by the Bonn Department of Education, interviewed 1,460 former Waldorf students born in the years of 1946 and 1947 and reached prevailingly positive findings in favour of the Waldorf schools. Their students have achieved, so the examiners have discovered, 'an educational plateau well above average'. The results appear to be formulated conservatively. For it is just this achievement of the Waldorf schools that holds surprises for the educational policy-makers. Some 22 per cent of the students polled passed the *Abitur*[2] at their own Waldorf school – even back in the years 1966 and 1967, almost three times more than in the state schools. Moreover, 40 per cent of those polled, who had 'never attended any other school than a Waldorf school' from grade 1 through 13, passed the *Abitur*.

These statistics appear even more significant when the conditions under which the exams were taken are considered – for instance, the fact that 'the *Abitur* does not lie within the interests of Rudolf Steiner's pedagogy' as stated by Stefan Leber, Board member of the Association of Waldorf Schools.

Practically speaking, this means that the students are taught according to Waldorf guidelines during their 12 years at school and are not specially prepared for the diploma examination. Only in the voluntary 13th year[3] is the curriculum oriented toward the requirements of the state schools and the *Abitur*. On top of this, the exam itself was 'an altogether unfamiliar *Abitur* given under strictest conditions: all tests came from outside the school; the exam was monitored by a state team of examiners'. Proponents of the conventional school system must be irritated by such results, because, after all, the Waldorf School is a *Gesamtschule* (see definition in the first paragraph) of the purest type. Nevertheless, it is now proven, says Bernhard Vier, who headed the research team, that 'among the students who were taught for 12 years on a non-selective basis, an even higher percentage are able to pass the *Abitur*'. 'The academicians have never wanted to believe that all this was possible', says Vier.

The Waldorf students showed a preference for occupations in the educational and social fields (20 per cent), in the medical field (12 per cent), and in the artistic/linguistic field (12 per cent); legal and technical professions were 'underrepresented'.[4] The graduates obviously took their incentives for professional choice from Waldorf values. Success, prestige, recognition, and career potential and income played at best a subordinate role. As 'personally especially important' in making their decision, the graduates named, above all, their own inclinations and abilities, independence and interest, followed by social and altruistic aspects.

Notes

[1]   A term used for the policy of allowing only the fittest to continue and leaving the others behind.

[2]   An examination whose equivalent in the United States would allow a student to skip introductory courses and, in effect, start college as a sophomore.

[3]   The US and German school systems are different from one another. American Waldorf schools have no voluntary 13th year; nor, of course, do the students have to take an *Abitur* examination.

[4]   Available American statistics are somewhat different. In 1986 Kimberton Waldorf School conducted a survey of its own high school alumni. Of those responding, 23 per cent were active in corporate or private business; 22 per cent had entered scientific, technological, or medical professions; and 16 per cent had become educators. The remaining responses showed that 16 per cent were active in the arts, theatre, or journalism, and 10 per cent had gone into the legal profession.

(Translation by Renate Field)
Compiled by the Admissions Office
Kimberton Waldorf School
Kimberton, PA 19442, USA

Appendix 3: The Hawthorn 'Early Years' Series – Holistic Parenting and Learning for Early Childhood

by Richard House, Series Editor

> There are parents... who are defying the directives of their culture. Such parents are not only helping their children to have a childhood... Those parents... will help to keep alive a human tradition. [Our culture] is halfway toward forgetting that children need childhood. Those who insist on remembering shall perform a noble service.
>
> Neil Postman[1]

Introduction

Neil Postman's resounding championing of childhood could hardly provide a more fitting epigraph for the Hawthorn Press 'Early Years' series. In the original version of this appendix,[2] I described the new series, set out its rationale, and commented upon more general cultural and educational issues that concern today's parents and early years professionals. In this updated version I will extend the discussion to take account of more recent literature and developments in the early years field.

The books in this series, which was founded in the millennial year 2000 with Russell Evans's well received *Helping Children to Overcome*

Fear, collectively provide a welcome and much-needed antidote to the prevailing British (and Western?) early-years ethos of over-active, prematurely intellectual intrusion into the young child's world – with, for example, its relentlessly mechanistic developmental assessments, compulsive over-testing and centrally dictated 'Early Learning Goals'. Yet the books in the series also offer their readers many practical insights into a whole range of early years-related questions and issues. Overall, then, the books in the Early Years series have a focus which is holistic, informed and practical – offering readers state-of-the-art information for those involved with young children who live and/or work in early years settings (i.e. from birth to about 6 years), be they familial or professional.

Ready to Learn in context

> Certainly there are needed right-hemisphere skills [that are] left undeveloped in education... There may be something to the notion that there needs to be more right-brain development in schools... It is *when* the hemispheres become competent at dealing with the world that matters.
>
> Robert Ornstein[3]

The most up-to-date research on learning and the brain is beginning to confirm the insights about learning that Rudolf Steiner offered to us nearly a century ago. To take just one example, Steiner's invocation to teach 'from the whole to the part' (rather than 'atomistically' from the part to the whole) is amply confirmed by neuro-psychologist Robert Ornstein when he recently writes that, in education, 'We should emphasize more of a top-down approach – ...*first teaching the overall framework*... We don't need a special right-brain learning program, but *simply to put the large picture first in front of the student*'.[4]

In this book Michael Rose and Martyn Rawson draw upon insights such as these to develop a systematic description of the main developmental processes involved in early learning and development, which in turn lay the essential foundation for later, more formal learning – or *school readiness*. *Ready to Learn* is a natural accompaniment to, and can profitably be read in conjunction with, several earlier books in the series – in particular Lynne Oldfield's *Free to Learn* and Sally Jenkinson's *The Genius of Play*.

Rudolf Steiner (on whose educational and developmental insights the authors' unfolding narrative substantially draws) embraced what is now widely termed a *Goethean approach* to science, an increasingly common methodology which privileges direct access to reality through the wisdom of personal experience and spiritual insight (e.g. see Henri Bortoft's book *The Wholeness of Nature: Goethe's Way of Science*, Floris, 1996). It is an approach which the authors implicitly adopt in this book, favouring knowledge gained through personal experience, insight and accumulated wisdom about child development, rather than through so-called 'objective' research and positivistically derived data.

The authors also eschew the fashionable 'everyone shall win prizes' approach to the question of early years learning. Rudolf Steiner was quite explicit about the actual physical and psychological harm that can be done to children by inappropriate early years educational experience, and recent trends in mainstream early years learning environments have been profoundly deleterious from a Steiner Waldorf or 'holistic' perspective. Certainly, in today's 'hyper-modernised' world, the damaging pressures on young children are relentless and ever-increasing. Anne Atkins, for example, recently described her routine experience of children *as young as three* being tested for entry into pre-schools;[5] and in a recent TES report, we read that

> Parents' fears… are fuelling a huge rise in private tuition, *particularly for primary-aged and pre-school children*… Parents spend around £100 million a year on personal tutors. *Some of this is spent on two-year-olds.* 'We have had a lot more enquiries about tuition for pupils preparing for key stage 1 and 2 national tests', said a spokeswoman for the Personal Tutors Agency… One child aged two-and-a-half received help from a Stepping Stones tutor. *The toddler had to point to his name on the blackboard and hone social skills to win a private nursery school place.*
>
> Top Tutors, a London-based agency… said it had frequent requests from parents of two-year-olds for help, although it refused to take children under three…[6]

Of course it is important not to impugn the motives of other approaches (e.g. to imply that they are somehow *deliberately* setting out to harm children) – for that would be patently absurd. Rather, this is a cultural, or *Zeitgeist* question rather than an exclusively personal one – and current mainstream approaches can legitimately be challenged at this 'world-view' level. Rose and Rawson's challenges to the mainstream are, then, a telling commentary on what are, arguably, *substantially incommensurable world-views about human development*, rather than direct personal criticisms of those implicated in mainstream policy-making.

Professor David Elkind[7] has also pointed out that children are *not* 'mini-adults', and are positively harmed through having to cope with age-inappropriate demands. It is upon such crucial developmental insights that Rudolf Steiner's original indications for Steiner Waldorf education were based – an education which has subsequently grown into a worldwide holistic educational movement (see 'Resources' section). Nobel Prize-winning physicist Murray Gell-Mannis is more specific about the harm caused by an unbalanced education:

> an elementary school program narrowly restricted to reading, writing, and arithmetic will educate mainly one hemisphere [of the brain], leaving half of an individual's high-level potential unschooled. Has our society tended to overemphasize the values of an analytical attitude, or even of logical reasoning? Perhaps in our educational system we lay too little emphasis on natural history.[8]

In sum, this, the sixth book in the Early Years series, sets a fitting tone for the series as a whole – drawing as it does upon perennial wisdom about, and penetrating observations of, child development; emphasising the crucial importance of expression through free play; and explicitly recognising the importance of the emotional and spiritual dimensions of human development.

The Hawthorn Early Years Series

The principal focus of the Early Years series is the promotion of healthy child development in its physical, emotional and spiritual dimensions. Each book arises from parents' own pressing questions and concerns about their children, such as: 'Why is creative play important?'; 'How can I tell when my child is ready to start formal schooling?'; 'How can I help sick children?'; 'How can I learn to be a family story-teller?'; 'What is distinctive about Steiner Waldorf early childhood education?'; 'How can I most effectively nourish my young child's experience of music in the early years?'; 'What effective "holistic" approaches are available for special needs children?' – and so on. The series is therefore very much driven by the experience of parents themselves, rather than being primarily professionally or 'expert'-driven, as is much of the early years literature.

The distinctive approach represented in these books is strongly, but not exclusively, informed by the flourishing world-wide network of some 1,500 Steiner-Waldorf kindergartens, and the 75 years of accumulated wisdom on child development that this global movement has built up – founded on the original work of the educationalist Dr Rudolf Steiner. The series freely draws upon the wisdom and insight of other prominent holistic approaches, including Froebel, Montessori and other respected holistic early years specialists. It thus embraces the emerging 'company of like-minded friends' (to adapt a phrase coined by series author and early years Waldorf specialist Sally Jenkinson), working together in their distinct yet complementary ways for healthy child development.

A defining feature of each book is its focus on a specific topic or question for which parents, teachers or other early years workers commonly require sound information and effective practical input. The series will also encompass Special Needs questions and children's needs for healing, as well as parents' and professionals' own needs for personal and spiritual growth and meaning.

Each book is based on up-to-date research and practice, and is written by an authority in the field in question. Hawthorn Press is working in close association and consultation with a range of parent educational organisations in the development of the series – for example, Parentline Plus and Winston's Wish, the Steiner Waldorf Kindergarten movement and the Steiner Schools Fellowship, the Alliance for Childhood, and Human Scale Education. In this way, the issues that the series is covering are emerging organically from the concerns of parents and educators themselves in today's demanding and complex world.

Each book's broadly indicative title accurately describes the book's purpose – for example, *Helping Children to Overcome Fear* by Russell

Evans; *Storytelling with Children* by Nancy Mellon; *The Genius of Play* by Sally Jenkinson; *Free to Learn – Introducing Steiner Waldorf Early Childhood Education* by Lynne Oldfield; and the current volume, *Ready to Learn* by Michael Rose and Martyn Rawson, among others. Each book contains Resources and Further Reading sections so that interested readers can follow up their interest in or commitment to the field in question. Future books are envisaged on such prescient issues as: movement and early learning; child development in holistic perspective; music in the early years; Special Needs questions; holistic baby care; creativity and the imagination in early childhood; and a cross-disciplinary anthology on play that builds upon Sally Jenkinson's seminal book, *The Genius of Play*.

The books in the series are already proving to be ideal 'study texts' for reading, study and support groups, as well as authoritative sources for holistic perspectives on early years training courses of all kinds. Finally, many of the books in this series promise to become *the* definitive works in their particular fields for many years to come, and have already received wide-ranging acclaim from a broad range of sources.

Discussion: The Early Years Debate in Context

In recent years there has been a rapidly growing interest in so-called 'new paradigm' thinking in a whole range of fields, including the natural sciences; and the impulse underlying this new series coheres closely with this developing 'trans-modern', post-materialistic world view. Parents and early years professionals alike are voicing ever more disquiet about prevailing cultural and educational challenges to childhood; and it is in this context that the Hawthorn Early Years series aims to disseminate more holistic values to a public which is increasingly seeking a humane and demonstrably effective alternative to what is currently on offer.

The distorting effects of anxiety on healthy development and learning, and the developmental dangers entailed in premature intellectual or ego development, are themes which recur throughout the series. The crucial role of free play is emphasised by a number of series authors: for, as Professor Tina Bruce said to the Anna Freud Centenary Conference in November 1995, 'Play cannot be pinned down and turned into a product of measurable learning. This is because play is a process [which] enables a holistic kind of learning, rather than fragmented learning'.

Relatedly, the young child needs an *unintruded-upon* space in which to play with, elaborate and work through her deepest wishes, anxieties and unconscious fantasies. In turn, the child will thereby gain competence in healthily managing – with her own freely developed will – her curiosities and anxieties about intersubjective experience and human relationship. Sally Jenkinson's Early Years book, *The Genius of Play*, develops these arguments at much greater length than I am able to here.

Another consistent theme is the pernicious deforming effects on young children of premature cognitive-intellectual development. As Professor Patrick Bateson and Paul Martin have written,[9] 'Children who are pushed too hard academically, and who consequently advance temporarily beyond their peers, may ultimately pay a price in terms of lost opportunities for development'. Certainly, some western governments seem narrowly preoccupied with an over-intrusive, control-obsessed modernity – leading to a child 'hot-housing' mentality which may well be harming a whole generation of children, as a recent UK Parliamentary Report has indicated.[10] Certainly, the inappropriate and highly damaging pressures on young children seem to be relentless and ever-increasing (cf. footnotes 5 and 6, above).

We are already witnessing signs of the harm being done by materialistic culture in general and by the current early years educational regime in particular. A recent study by the National Health Foundation[11] reports record levels of stress-related mental health problems in children. And in a recent press report,[12] the frightening scale of medically diagnosed child 'behavioural disorders' was highlighted, with 'tens of thousands of schoolchildren with mild behaviour problems [now] being drugged with Ritalin… simply in order to control them'. It is by no means far-fetched to propose some kind of causal relationship between the burgeoning and comparatively recent epidemic in child 'behavioural disturbances', and recent early years policy 'innovations' which demand a relentless and intrusive surveillance, measurement, assessment and testing of children's developmental processes – not to mention the forced imposition of premature, adult-centric cognitive-intellectual learning at ever-earlier ages.[13]

On this view, symptoms of so-called 'attention deficit disorder' are surely far better understood as children's understandable response to, and unwitting commentary on, technological culture's ever-escalating overstimulation – and not least, its cognitively-biased distortions of early child development. Until our policy-makers develop the insight to recognise and then respond to this malaise at a cultural level rather than at an individualised medical level, the prevalence of children's 'behavioural difficulties' will inevitably continue to escalate – Ritalin or no Ritalin.

Conclusion: Finding a Better Way

These, then, are just some of the themes that recur in this important book series. As I write (October 2001), there is a growing sense that the tide is now turning against those pernicious cultural forces that have been systematically 'dismembering' childhood – and towards a re-membering of a holistic, humanistic vision of childhood which sees the damage that is being wrought by modern culture, and which offers practical and effective alternatives. To take just a few examples: both Ulster and Wales have recently (2001) decided to scrap school league performance tables, and Welsh Assembly Education Minister Jane Davidson has recently been instrumental in relaxing the over-academic pressures in Welsh early years education. In England, too, a recent petition organised by early years consultant Margaret Edgington, and presented to the education minister in September 2001, gained well over a thousand signatures in support of the (admittedly limited) child-centred gains represented in the government's *Curriculum Guidance for the Foundation Stage* policy document – gains which are coming under increasing threat from a number of sources (Margaret Edgington, personal communication). There are now even signs that British Education Ministers are starting to consider the possibility of a later start to formal schooling.[14] To the extent that the Hawthorn Early Years series can buttress and reinforce this mounting sea-change in attitudes to childhood, it will have more than served its purpose.

It is axiomatic that the key to building a better world lies in just how successfully we can facilitate our children's healthy development. Our aim in this series is indeed to provide a rich range of books which will 'help parents defy the directives of modern culture' (Postman), and *find a better way* to raise their children and help them realise their full potential. The books which we publish help parents and professionals to *reinvigorate* the rapidly disappearing art of *understanding children and their developmental needs*, which modern materialist culture has done so much to undermine.

Above all, the authors in the Early Years series would all surely agree that education should nourish and facilitate, rather than subvert, children's innate *love of learning*[15] – as Ornstein has it:

> We're confronted with a large number of students and educators dissatisfied with the emphasis on drilling unrelated facts. Students [and children] lose interest, they don't see the relevance to their life... We're trained for drills and learning things without connecting them to the world.[16]

And there seems little doubt that in the era of modernity, education has become unhelpfully skewed towards 'left-brain' learning, which emphasises *the detail* – i.e. 'the small elements of a worldview..., linking them tightly together so they can be acted upon, produced, reproduced, like a formula' – to the neglect of *overall context* – i.e. 'right-brain' learning, with its specialisation for 'the large strokes of a life's portrait...', where the parts fit the context of our life',[17] conveying emphases, subtext and contextual meaning. One can hardly exaggerate just what is at stake in all this – for as Robert Ornstein writes,

> We've built a world that often overwhelms our mind's native ability to manage. So our focus needs to shift from the smaller ones towards understanding the nature of the larger systems in which we live.[18]

And it is in this context that holistically inclined, genuinely balanced learning, along the lines outlined in Rose and Rawson's excellent book, clearly becomes an absolute necessity for the future well-being of our modern world.

In closing, we invite you to support this important series – and in so doing, to join the rapidly growing body of parents and educators who are determined to explore different ways.

Richard House
Norwich, England
October 2001

Notes

1   From his important book *The Disappearance of Childhood.*
2   In R. Evans, *Helping Children to Overcome Fear*, pp. 91-9.
3   R. Ornstein, *The Right Mind*, pp. 96, 150 (original emphasis).
4   Ibid., pp. 171, 172 (emphasis added).
5   'Thought for the Day', BBC Radio 4 'Today' programme, 3 October 2001, and personal communication.
6   S. Kirkman, 'Parents fears trigger private tuition boom' (emphases added).
7   From his book *Ties that Stress: The New Family Imbalance* (Harvard University Press, 1994).
8   Quoted in Ornstein, *The Right Mind*, p. 170.
9   In their *Design for Life: How Behaviour Develops* (Cape, 1999).
10 See G. Hackett, 'Early handwriting may be harmful', *Times Educational Supplement*, 9 June 2000, p. 14.
11 J. Tweed, 'Mental health problems rise in all children'. See also E. Hartley-Brewer's *Learning to Trust and Trusting to Learn*, and R. Smithers, 'Exams regime "harms pupils"'.
12 A. Browne, 'Mind-control drug threat for children'.
13 See, for example, R. House, 'Whatever happened to holism?: *Curriculum Guidance for the Foundation Stage* – a Critique'.
14 T. Halpin, 'Children can start school at six, says new Minister'.
15 R. House, 'Loving to learn'.
16 Ornstein, *The Right Brain*, pp. 170, 171.
17 Ibid., p. 162.
18 Ibid, p. 172.

Holistic Perspectives on Child Learning: References & Further Reading

Alliance for Childhood (2000) *Fool's Gold: A Critical Look at Computers in Childhood*, College Park, Md

Baldwin Dancy, R. (2000) *You Are Your Child's First Teacher*, 2nd edn, Celestial Arts, Berkeley, Calif.

Brown, T., Foot, M. and Holt, P. (2001) *Let Our Children Learn: Allowing Ownership, Providing Support, Celebrating Achievement*, Education Now Books, Nottingham (from 113 Arundel Drive, Bramcote Hills, Nottingham NG9 3FQ)

Browne, A. (2000) 'Mind-control drug threat for children', *The Observer* newspaper, 27 February, pp.1, 2

Charter, D. (1998) 'Early learning may put boys off school', *The Times* newspaper, 24 March, p. 8

Coles, J. (2000) 'Hyper-parenting: are we pushing our children too hard?', *The Times* newspaper, 'Times 2' Supplement, pp. 3-4

DeGrandpre, R. (2000) *Ritalin Nation: Rapid-Fire Culture and the Transformation of Human Consciousness*, W. W. Norton, New York

Elkind, D. (1981) *The Hurried Child: Growing Up Too Fast Too Soon*, Addison-Wesley, Reading, Mass.

Elkind, D. (1987) *Mis-education: Pre-schoolers at Risk*, A. A. Knopf, New York

Elkind, D. (1990) 'Academic pressures – too much, too soon: the demise of play', in E. Klugman and S. Smilansky (eds), *Children's Play and Learning: Perspectives and Policy Implications*, Teachers College Press, Columbia University, New York, 1990, pp. 3-17

Evans, R. (2000) *Helping Children to Overcome Fear: The Healing Power of Play*, Hawthorn Press, Stroud

Haller, I. (1991) *How Children Play*, Floris Books, Edinburgh

Halpin, T. (2001) 'Children can start school at six, says new Minister', *Daily Mail*, 28 June, p. 17.

Hartley-Brewer, E. (2001) *Learning to Trust and Trusting to Learn*, Institute for Public Policy Research, London (www.ippr.org.uk)

Healy, J. M. (1990) *Endangered Minds: Why Children Don't Think and What We Can Do about It*, Touchstone/Simon & Schuster, New York

Healy, J. M. (1998) *Failure to Connect: How Computers Affect Our Children's Minds – for Better and Worse*, Simon & Schuster, New York

House, R. (2000) 'Psychology and early years learning: affirming the wisdom of Waldorf', *Steiner Education*, 34 (2), 10-16

House, R. (2001a) 'Loving to learn', *Natural Parent*, May/June, pp. 38-40

House, R. (2001b) 'Whatever happened to holism?: *Curriculum Guidance for the Foundation Stage* – a Critique', *Education Now: News and Review*, 33, p. 3

Institute for Public Policy Research (2001) 'Exam mania could scar children's emotional health', press release, 24 August (www.ippr.org.uk)

Jaffke, F. (2000) *Work and Play in Early Childhood*, Floris Books, Edinburgh

Jenkinson, S. (2001) *The Genius of Play: Celebrating the Spirit of Childhood*, Hawthorn Press, Stroud

Kirkman, S. (2001) 'Parents' fears trigger private tuition boom', *Times Educational Supplement*, 19 October, p. 1

Large, M. (1992) *Who's Bringing Them Up? How to Kick the TV Habit*, 2nd edition, Hawthorn Press, Stroud

Macintyre, C. (2001) *Enhancing Learning through Play: A Developmental Perspective for Early Years Settings*, David Fulton, London

Medved, M. & Medved, D. (1998) *Saving Childhood: Protecting Our Children from the National Assault on Innocence*, HarperCollins, Zondervan

Mills, D. and Mills, C. (1997) 'Britain's Early Years Disaster: Part 1 – The Findings', mimeograph

Moore, R. S. & Moore, D. N. (1975) *Better Late than Early: A New Approach to Your Child's Education*, Reader's Digest Press (Dutton), New York

Ornstein, R. (1997) *The Right Mind: Making Sense of the Hemispheres*, Harcourt Brace, New York

Patterson, B.J. and Bradley, P. (2000) *Beyond the Rainbow Bridge: Nurturing Our Children from Birth to Seven*, Michaelmas Press, Amesbury, Mass.

Postman, N. (1994) *The Disappearance of Childhood*, Vintage Books, New York

Professional Association of Teachers (2000) *Tested to Destruction? A Survey of Examination Stress in Teenagers*, PAT, London

Salter, J. (1987) *The Incarnating Child*, Hawthorn Press, Stroud

Sanders, B. (1995) *A is for Ox: The Collapse of Literacy and the Rise of Violence in an Electronic Age*, Vintage Books, New York

Schweinhart, L.J. and Weikart, D. P. (1997) *Lasting Differences: The High/Scope Preschool Curriculum Comparison Study through Age 23*, High/Scope Press, Ypsilanti, MI; Monographs of the High/Scope Educational Research Foundation No. 12

Sharp, C. (1998) 'Age of starting school and the early years curriculum', paper presented at the National Foundation for Educational Research Annual Conference, London, October (available at www.nfer.ac.uk/conferences/early.htm)

Smithers, R. (2000) 'Exams regime "harms pupils"', The *Guardian* newspaper, 4 August, p. 1

Steiner, R. (1995) *The Kingdom of Childhood*, Anthroposophic Press, Hudson, New York

Steiner Education (2000) Special Issue: 'Caring for Childhood: Waldorf and the Early Years Debate', Vol. 34, No. 2

Thomson, J. B. & others (1994) *Natural Childhood: A Practical Guide to the First Seven Years*, Gaia Books, London

Tweed, J. (2000) 'Mental health problems rise in all children', *Nursery World*, 6 April, pp. 8-9

Other books from Hawthorn Press

Storytelling with Children
Nancy Mellon

Telling stories awakens wonder and creates
special occasions with children. Nancy
Mellon shows how you can become a
confident storyteller and enrich your family
with the power of story.

192pp; 216 x 138mm; illustrations;
paperback; 1 903458 08 0

Muddles, Puddles and Sunshine
Your activity book to help
when someone has died.
Winston's Wish

*Muddles, Puddles and
Sunshine* offers practical and sensitive support for bereaved children.
It suggests a helpful series of activities and exercises accompanied by
the friendly characters of Bee and Bear.

32pp; 297 x 210mm landscape; illustrations; paperback; 1 869 890 58 2

Free to Learn
Introducing Steiner Waldorf early
childhood education
Lynne Oldfield

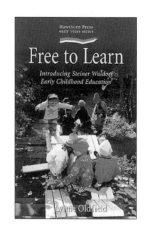

Free to Learn is a unique guide to the
principles and methods of Steiner
Waldorf early childhood education.
This authoritative introduction is
written by Lynne Oldfield, Director of
the London Steiner Waldorf Early
Childhood Teacher Training course.
She draws on kindergarten experience from around the world, with
stories, helpful insights, lively observations and pictures. This
inspiring book will interest parents, educators and early years
students. It is up to date, comprehensive, includes many photos
and has a 16 page colour section.

256pp; 216 x 138mm; photographs; paperback; 1 903458 06 4

Helping Children to Overcome Fear
The healing power of play
Russell Evans

Critical illness can cause overwhelming
feelings of abandonment and loss. Difficult for adults to face alone, for children
the experience is magnified. Jean Evans
was a play leader who recognised ahead
of her time the importance of enabling
children to give voice to their feelings, providing opportunities
for play and working in partnership with parents.

128pp; 216 x 138mm; paperback; 1 903458 02 1

The Genius of Play
Celebrating the spirit of childhood
Sally Jenkinson

Children move like quick fire from the fantastic to the everyday, when free to express the genius of play. *The Genius of Play* addresses what play is, why it matters, and how modern life endangers children's play. The secrets of play are explored from moving stories and research. Here is an outspoken Children's Play Charter for parents and teachers, which celebrates the playful spirit of childhood.

224pp; 216 x 138mm; paperback; 1 903458 04 8

Free Range Education
How home education works
Terri Dowty (ed)

Welcome to this essential handbook for families considering or starting out in home education. *Free Range Education* is full of family stories, resources, burning questions, humour, tips, practical steps and useful advice so you can choose what best suits your family situation. You are already your child's main teacher and these families show how home education can work for you. Both parents and children offer useful guidance, based on their experience.

256pp; 210 x 148mm; cartoons; paperback; 1 903458 07 2

Getting in touch with Hawthorn Press

What are your pressing questions about the early years?
The Hawthorn Early Years Series arises from parents' and educators' pressing questions and concerns – so please contact us with your questions. These will help spark new books, workshops or festivals if there is sufficient interest. We will be delighted to hear your views on our Early Years books, how they can be improved, and what your needs are.

Visit our website for details of the Early Years Series and forthcoming books and events:

http://www.hawthornpress.com

Ordering books

If you have difficulties ordering Hawthorn Press books from a bookshop, you can order direct from:

United Kingdom
Scottish Book Source Distribution,
137 Dundee Street, Edinburgh,
EH11 1BG
Tel: 0131 229 6800 Fax: 0131 229 9070

North America
Anthroposophic Press c/o Books International,
PO Box 960,
Herndon, VA 201 72-0960.
Toll free order line: 800-856-8664
Toll free fax line: 800-277-9747

Dear Reader

If you wish to follow up your reading of this book, please tick the boxes below as appropriate, fill in your name and address and return to Hawthorn Press:

☐ Please send me a catalogue of other Hawthorn Press books.

☐ Please send me details of Early Years events and courses.

Questions I have about the Early Years are:

_____

_____

_____

_____

_____

Name _____

Address _____

_____

_____

Postcode _____ Tel. no. _____

Please return to: Hawthorn Press, Hawthorn House,
1 Lansdown Lane, Stroud, Glos. GL5 1BJ, UK
or Fax (01453) 751138